THE ANSWER BOOK

FOR TROUBLED TIMES

by Holly Lewerenz

ISBN 978-0-615-32679-5
Second Printing

Author Contact Info: Holly Lewerenz
P.O. Box 31883, Chicago, IL 60631

Phone: (817) 285-0058

Email: Holly@HealingforAmerica.com
Websites: www.HealingforAmerica.com
www.JesusHealingHouse.org

Cover design by Morning Star Studio
Information available by writing:
P.O. Box 631843, Irving, TX 75063

Typeset by Susan Harring
Information available by e-mailing: harring87@att.net

Dedication

Jesus Christ is the beginning and the end of my life…my purpose for living, my strength, my Savior and Lord, and my all in all. I dedicate this book to Him!

Secondly, I dedicate this book to my sons, Dave Lewerenz and Rich Lewerenz, and my granddaughter, Autumn Lewerenz, all of whom are my joy, my inspiration, and the most important people in my life. I love you, Dave, Rich and Autumn, and pray that you will walk every day in the fullness of God's purpose and plan for your lives, trusting in Him alone…for the days are short and the coming of Jesus Christ is near.

Acknowledgement

I acknowledge the tireless and dedicated efforts and encouragement of my oldest son, Dave Lewerenz, who has been instrumental in the writing and compilation of this book. Dave is a news hound and a tremendous researcher, and I owe him a debt of gratitude for providing information and inspiration regarding the status of current events in the world today. Here is Dave's personal testimony about getting to know God:

ॐ   ॐ

"Like many others, I first learned about God, Jesus, heaven, being saved, etc... when I was around 10 years old. My mom had just gotten born-again and would bring my little brother and me to church. Within a few weeks I had accepted Jesus as my Savior and knew my sins were forgiven and I could now go to heaven... That was the easy part! The hard part (or so I thought) back then was now I had to try really hard to be good all the time and follow the Ten Commandments, otherwise God would get angry with me and bad things would happen!

Needless to say, around age 12 I really started to rebel against my mom, teachers, deacons, police, etc... typical of most kids that are trying to be more independent and grown up. But since I couldn't follow the Ten Commandments, I became angry with God... not knowing at that time that the Ten Commandments were a guide to show unsaved people their inability to be good and why they needed Jesus in order to get into heaven. In hindsight, I now know that it is by learning to love people and by walking closer to God that sin becomes less and less natural to do and righteousness more and more natural to do automatically!

(continued on next page)

(continued from previous page)

So while inside I was ticked off at God, I kept reading about the "Last Days"... you know... the antichrist, the "666" mark, the wars and rumors of wars, etc.... Over the last 20 some odd years that I was away from God, He kept the Last Days info in my mind. Then in October 2007, my brother was telling me about the Masons and how they influence everything in society and I got curious. As I researched, I came across Presidential Candidate Ron Paul talking about globalism, how American policy had been hijacked, and various other topics.

Over the next few weeks the Holy Spirit was working hard to show me how what Ron Paul and others were warning against was part of the foundation being laid for the antichrist system! I soon recommitted my life to Jesus Christ and have learned so much more about life and what following God is really about... in a nutshell... It's all about realizing we are like little kids that must learn to trust our "Dad," knowing that God is truly good and will provide for us... That we are literally learning a new way to live and have to unlearn all the bad habits, which takes time... The closer we get to God and viewing Him like a father, the more of His goodness and love that flows out. On the flip side, the more we worry about the bad we still do, the farther we stray away from God and consequentially, the more bad we do!

Thanks be to God / "Dad" for His awesome patience, kindness and wisdom... and no doubt His protection through those 20 years... allowing me the time and opportunity to get to know Him as He originally intended."

Dave Lewerenz

Table of Contents

Foreword

We are living in an incredible day that was foretold in the Bible thousands of years ago. This is the most critical time of financial crisis, famine, natural disasters, fear and untold misery for millions of people on planet earth. People are looking to the government, the media, education, science, the medical field for the solutions—almost everywhere—but to the Creator Himself.

THE ANSWER BOOK for Troubled Times by Holly Lewerenz is right on time.

This book addresses the urgent issues facing America today with an honest evaluation, yet places the blame on no one person or political party. Holly shares the true and only Answer with everyone: Americans, the Church, Moslems, and every person who is sincerely seeking answers to the imminent dangers we face as a nation—and as a world in crisis.

However *THE ANSWER BOOK for Troubled Times* is not a doomsday book by any means. It offers hope and concrete, practical ideas for turning America around and for protecting you and your family in the midst of chaos.

In Psalms 37:18-19 (AMP), the Word of God says:

> *The Lord knows the days of the upright and blameless, and their heritage will abide forever. They shall not be put to shame in the time of evil; and in the days of famine they shall be satisfied.*

(continued on next page)

(continued from previous page)

Yes, there is hope! God will take care of every person who places their trust in Him. I recommend reading and sharing with others this timely, important book for today: *THE ANSWER BOOK for Troubled Times.*

This book will be a real guide to anyone truly seeking the FINAL ANSWER!

Dr. Morris Cerullo
President
Morris Cerullo World Evangelism

Dr. Morris Cerullo is a worldwide evangelist whose prophetic and teaching ministry has covered much of the globe for over 67 years. In addition to conducting both national and international schools of ministry and conferences, Dr. Cerullo hosts a television program: *Victory Today!* For more information about Dr. Cerullo's ministry, complimentary magazine *Blessed*, books, DVDs and CDs, please feel free to visit his website at www.mcwe.com.

Chapter One

A Wake Up Call: Do You Recognize the Signs of the Times?

U.S., Iranian Tensions Continue to Mount

(Fox News, January 4, 2012)

25 dead, 100 missing in Philippine landslide

(ABC News, January 5, 2012)

IDF: 8,000 rockets, missiles could hit Israel if war erupts

(Jerusalem Post, January 3, 2012)

Iowa same-sex parents win birth certificate lawsuit

(USA Today, January 5, 2012)

Banks warn on lending as euro crisis raises costs

(The Telegram (UK), January 5, 2012)

As originally written in mid-2008 prior to the U.S. presidential election won by then-Illinois Senator, Barack Obama, you will find that some of the key insights in *THE ANSWER BOOK for Troubled Times* have already begun to ring prophetically true. Though most of the content in this book, however; remains untouched from its original writing, the preceding news headlines and related information have been updated to reflect current events.

We are once again in an American presidential election year. At this writing, GOP hopefuls are debating conservative, constitutional and moderate ideologies in their quest to win the Republican primary and become their party's candidate to run against seated President, Barack Obama.

Whatever the outcome, we are definitely living in critical, yet exciting, times and I'm sure you will agree: America – and the world – need a new, positive direction to take us from our current, dismal outlook of uncertainty to a future of hope and stability.

You will find thoughts and information herein that will likely cause your heart to skip a beat, but I want to assure you that this book is not written to cause fear or worry in those who read it. On the contrary, its purpose is to bring hope, peace, and a committed effort on the part of Americans to work together to enjoy and prosper in a nation in which we can be proud to live and work…a nation that will once again earn the respect of other nations worldwide.

Though times look bad and uncertainty prevails everywhere, there is hope—and there are answers, if we will but honestly seek them and accept the truth...

I am an American and I love my country. This book is written with no intent to criticize people, places or things, but with the desire to alerting all who will listen to become aware and take notice that the events which are happening today in the United States of America and around the world are not coincidental nor are they the result of which political party is in office. Today's dilemmas are not the fault of the Republicans...the Democrats...or of any particular political agenda.

Former President Ronald Reagan said, "If we ever forget that we are one nation under God, then we will be a nation gone under."

What does it say in the Bible about the leadership of a nation?

"Blessed in the nation whose God is the Lord..."
(Psalm 33:12, NKJV)

A few dictionary definitions for the word "blessed" are as follows:
(*Dictionary.com Unabridged (v1.1)*)
3. divinely or supremely favored; fortunate: *to be blessed with a strong, healthy body, blessed with an ability to find friends.*
4. blissfully happy or contented.

6. bringing happiness and thankfulness: *the blessed assurance of a steady income.*

Wow! America can be highly favored, having fortune (prosperity), blissfully happy and contented. Look especially at definition number six. Not only can America be all of these things that make up the definition of the word "blessed," we can bring that blessing to others when God rules our country.

> *Righteousness exalts a nation, but sin is a disgrace to any people.*
>
> (Proverbs 14:34, NIV)

Being "blessed" carries with it a responsibility. God did not send Jesus to be the Savior only, but Lord of those who have received His salvation. When God the Father and Jesus the Son are ruling in the lives of a majority of Americans, we can't help it but walk in righteousness…a true goodness and "rightness—a right way" of doing things. A result of walking in this kind of righteousness is honor. I pray for the day when America has honor, not disgrace, among the nations. She will, if her people heed the warnings of Jesus to repent and turn back to God.

Time is short!

There is not much time left to make this decision. The days are critical…conditions are critical…whether they look like it or not! Are we living in the end times? Yes! Do you know that when you read Bible prophecy, you are reading tomorrow's news headlines today? Look at these words spoken by Jesus to His followers, over two thousand years ago, when they asked what the signs would be upon the earth in the closing days of this age:

1 As Jesus was leaving the Temple grounds, his disciples pointed out to him the various Temple buildings.

2 But he responded, "Do you see all these buildings? I tell you the truth, they will be completely demolished. Not one stone will be left on top of another!"

3 Later, Jesus sat on the Mount of Olives. His disciples came to him privately and said, "Tell us, when will all this happen? What sign will signal your return and the end of the world?"

4 Jesus told them, "Don't let anyone mislead you,

5 for many will come in my name, claiming, 'I am the Messiah.' They will deceive many.

6 And you will hear of wars and threats of wars, but don't panic. Yes, these things must take place, but the end won't follow immediately.

7 Nation will go to war against nation, and kingdom against kingdom. There will be famines and earthquakes in many parts of the world.

8 But all this is only the first of the birth pains, with more to come.

9 "Then you will be arrested, persecuted, and killed. You will be hated all over the world because you are my followers.

15

10 And many will turn away from me and betray and hate each other.

11 And many false prophets will appear and will deceive many people.

12 Sin will be rampant everywhere, and the love of many will grow cold.

13 But the one who endures to the end will be saved.

14 And the Good News about the Kingdom will be preached throughout the whole world, so that all nations will hear it; and then the end will come.

15 "The day is coming when you will see what Daniel the prophet spoke about—the sacrilegious object that causes desecration standing in the Holy Place." (Reader, pay attention!)

16 "Then those in Judea must flee to the hills.

17 A person out on the deck of a roof must not go down into the house to pack.

18 A person out in the field must not return even to get a coat.

19 How terrible it will be for pregnant women and for nursing mothers in those days.

20 And pray that your flight will not be in winter or on the Sabbath.

21 For there will be greater anguish than at any time since the world began. And it will never be so great again.

22 In fact, unless that time of calamity is shortened, not a single person will survive. But it will be shortened for the sake of God's chosen ones.

23 "Then if anyone tells you, 'Look, here is the Messiah,' or 'There he is,' don't believe it.

24 For false messiahs and false prophets will rise up and perform great signs and wonders so as to deceive, if possible, even God's chosen ones.

25 See, I have warned you about this ahead of time.

26 "So if someone tells you, 'Look, the Messiah is out in the desert,' don't bother to go and look. Or, 'Look, he is hiding here,' don't believe it!

27 For as the lightning flashes in the east and shines to the west, so it will be when the Son of Man comes.

28 Just as the gathering of vultures shows there is a carcass nearby, so these signs indicate that the end is near.

*29 "Immediately after the anguish of those days, the sun will be darkened,
the moon will give no light,
the stars will fall from the sky,
and the powers in the heavens will be shaken.*

30 And then at last, the sign that the Son of Man is coming will appear in the heavens, and there will be deep mourning among all the peoples of the earth. And they will see the Son of Man coming on the clouds of heaven with power and great glory.

31 And he will send out his angels with the mighty blast of a trumpet, and they will gather his chosen ones from all over the world—from the farthest ends of the earth and heaven.

32 "Now learn a lesson from the fig tree. When its branches bud and its leaves begin to sprout, you know that summer is near.

33 In the same way, when you see all these things, you can know his return is very near, right at the door.

34 I tell you the truth, this generation will not pass from the scene until all these things take place.

35 Heaven and earth will disappear, but my words will never disappear.

36 "However, no one knows the day or hour when these things will happen, not even the angels in heaven or the Son himself. Only the Father knows.

37 "When the Son of Man returns, it will be like it was in Noah's day.

38 In those days before the flood, the people were enjoying banquets and parties and weddings right up to the time Noah entered his boat.

39 People didn't realize what was going to happen until the flood came and swept them all away. That is the way it will be when the Son of Man comes.

40 "Two men will be working together in the field; one will be taken, the other left.

41 Two women will be grinding flour at the mill; one will be taken, the other left.

42 "So you, too, must keep watch! For you don't know what day your Lord is coming.

43 Understand this: If a homeowner knew exactly when a burglar was coming, he would keep watch and not permit his house to be broken into.

44 You also must be ready all the time, for the Son of Man will come when least expected.

(Matthew 24:1-44, NLT)

A sure word of prophecy

Noted Bible expert, Dr. Jack Van Impe and his wife Rexella, have a wonderful television program on Bible prophecy. (Look for *Jack Van Impe Presents* in your local TV listings or you can contact them at www.JVIM.com for more information.) Dr. Van Impe comments in his video *Prophecy 21st Century Revelations* that there are 10,385 verses on Bible prophecy—the things to come—out of a total 165,000 Scripture verses in the Bible itself. This means that one out of every 16 Bible verses is prophetic. Dr. Van Impe further states that there are 300 prophecies on the first coming of Christ, with a 20 to 1 ratio of prophecies concerning the second coming of Christ. That's 6,000 prophecies that tell us Jesus is coming again—and He's coming soon! These prophecies are found not only in the book of Revelation, but in the Old Testament prophets as well and in the New Testament, for example in the passages of Matthew 24 that we just read.

Jesus warned His disciples about the things to come that would precede His coming to earth for them—and for all true believers of every age. Do you recognize some of these signs? Earthquakes, wars and rumors of wars, famines, plagues and more?

Natural disasters, such as earthquakes, hurricanes, tsunamis, monsoons, tornadoes and cyclones, cover the earth. In 2011, the most powerful known earthquake ever to hit Japan, and one of the five most powerful earthquakes in the world, resulted in a death toll of approximately 20,000 lives. Apart from this tragic human loss, the financial loss was incomparable. The World Bank's estimated economic cost for this tsunami was US$235 billion, making it the most expensive natural disaster on record. In 2010, a horrific earthquake in Haiti killed 316,000 people, injured 300,000, and a million more became homeless. Prior to this, a devastating tsunami hit Indonesia, killing over 350,000 people; also earthquakes in Kashmir killed between 100,000 to 150,000; in Pakistan killed more than 86,000, and in China killed almost 70,000 people. Earthquakes, though minor, even rocked places like Texas and Oklahoma recently, which are not geographical areas where you usually expect to encounter earthquakes. Hurricane Katrina in the southeast portion of the United States in 2005 was the most costly natural disaster ever in America and the deadliest since 1929. Almost 2,000 people died in Louisiana and neighboring states, and 1.2 million residents were displaced from their homes.

Famines are rampant over the world too, and have been for centuries. Famine has struck many Asian and African countries including Sudan; Somalia; Burma; North Korea, where the media reported that more than 40% of Korean children were severely malnourished; Ethiopia, where 4.5 million children were reported to be facing starvation, Somalia, and others. Hunger has increased in the United States also, and I believe may become a major problem in America as unemployment continues, food prices rise and food shortages result. Additional causes for worldwide famine have included war, floods and other natural disasters.

A day's pay buys one loaf of bread!

In these times, the economic climate will become so bad that the Bible says a single loaf of bread will cost an entire day's wages. In chapter six of the book of Revelation, the famous four horsemen of the Apocalypse are described. The third one gives a glimpse of this coming escalation of economical pressure:

> *When the Lamb broke the third seal, I heard the third living being say, "Come!" I looked up and saw a black horse, and its rider was holding a pair of scales in his hand. And I heard a voice from among the four living beings say, "A loaf of wheat bread or three*

*loaves of barley will cost a day's pay. And
don't waste the olive oil and wine."*

(Revelation 6:5-6, NLT)

It is no longer business as usual! Current events are setting the scene for the fulfillment of Bible prophecy—God's plan for these end times of the world as we know it. We've already seen droughts, famines and shortages around the world. Shortage of oil, and its resulting increases in cost, have endangered the world's fuel supply. Corn, wheat and other grains have been in short supply, causing the cost of groceries to sky-rocket. When you go to your local supermarket, even the "sale" prices are higher now than the regular prices that were formerly the norm. As a result of increased fuel and food costs, the cost of living is rising substantially while employee wages remain the same and the value of houses and other property declines rapidly and severely.

Throughout America it has become almost impossible for homeowners to sell their houses for anywhere near what they were previously worth and many now owe on their mortgages amounts above their currently appraised property values.

One look at the "Help Wanted" ads in the local newspaper or in online job listings will show the fear and caution existing in today's job market. Employers are cutting back wherever possible, raises and new hiring are being "frozen" because of the uncertainty of the economy. The unemployed person is finding it difficult to obtain work because the previous pages of dozens and dozens of open jobs have dwindled down to a few, and along with corporation and even small business layoffs, the competition for available jobs is fierce.

Retail is down in sales throughout almost every sector despite the government's efforts to jumpstart the economy through billions of dollars in corporate bailouts and controversial payroll tax cuts.

Disillusioned American citizens joined the "Occupy" movement, an international protest movement, which was primarily directed against economic and social inequality. The first Occupy protest to receive wide news coverage was "Occupy Wall Street" in New York City, which began during September, 2011. By early October, Occupy protests had taken place or were ongoing in over 95 cities across 82 nations worldwide and in over 600 communities in the United States alone. By the end of the year, an "Occupy" web page listed almost 3,000 Occupy communities worldwide. Assembling together in public parks, streets and other venues, the "Occupiers" were dispersed and some were arrested by police in one city after another. As of the end of the year, despite winter's bitter weather conditions and the opposition of local authorities, this movement showed no signs of letting up.

Jesus came to save, not to condemn!

Having said all this, I want to assure you though that, even in the face of how things may look, GOD IS NOT MAD AT AMERICA!

For God so loved the world that He gave His only begotten Son, that whoever believes in Him should not perish but have everlasting life. For God did not send His Son into the world to condemn the world, but that the world through Him might be saved.

(John 3:16-17, NKJV)

If you are a parent, or even if you are not, you can probably imagine with me the vilest, meanest person you know or can picture. Someone who has treated you wrong and caused you much pain. Now, you have a child whom you love dearly, who has done nothing to deserve punishment, but yet instead of taking out your wrath on that person who has done evil to you, you punish your own dear son or daughter in that other person's place. Your son or daughter suffers unfathomable misery, even unto death, but the evil one goes free, forgiven, and never having to pay back or make up for what he did wrong.

This is what God (the Father) did for you and me through His Son, Jesus! That's how much He loves you and wants to have a relationship with you. Yes, the great God of the universe wants to be your Friend! He didn't send His Son to die for you so that you would have to follow a bunch of rules and regulations, but so that you could be free in His power and strength to live a rewarding and meaningful life. Some think that if they turn to Christ, they will be bored and sent off to the jungles in Africa or somewhere equally unfamiliar. But, friend, let me tell you; the Christian life is the most exciting adventure you'll find anywhere.

God has a custom plan designed just for you that fits your personality, your interests, and your skills. Don't forget the gifts that are in you come from God; they are not just abilities you randomly cultivated all on your own. Getting even more basic than that, we could not do anything at all, apart from God who gives us our daily breath…and bread!

Why does God allow people to suffer?

The question often comes up, "Well, if God is so good, why does He let little children be molested and innocent people be hit by a drunken motorist or washed away in a horrible hurricane?" The answer is simple. When God created the earth, He populated it with one man and one woman, to whom He gave dominion over its resources and the daily matters of life. In other words, God gave Adam and Eve, and every human being since then, freedom of CHOICE. Yes, God is pro-choice, but His choices are always good, always in favor of life, health, prosperity, and everything good!

God did make one stipulation; however, and most of you have probably read the story and know that there was one tree in the beautiful, lush garden of Eden that was forbidden to God's man and woman. The tree of the knowledge of good and evil. When they disobediently ate of the fruit of that tree, Adam and Eve's eyes and understanding were opened no longer only to good, but to evil. That choice has set the stage for all the wrong choices… all the painful choices…all the foolish choices that man has ever made since.

At that point, Adam and Eve allowed the evil serpent, the devil, to influence them and to take over the dominion of the world that God meant for them to possess. So to answer the question, "Why does God allow evil?" I would say, "He doesn't!" Evil does not come from God; it comes from the devil. Evil is not allowed to operate in this world by God; it is allowed to operate by the man and woman, who have allowed it into their lives and environment personally, and through the original sin of Adam and Eve, which became the sin nature of all human beings. Though Adam and Eve were the ones who allowed sin into the world, each of us individually have sinned and fallen short of the glory of God in some way. It doesn't have to be murder or adultery; sins also include little white lies, gossip, even fear of man and unbelief toward God.

"Can't God stop the evil…the pain…the tragedy?" Yes, of course He can. God is sovereign and can do ALL things. And, sometimes He does! How many times have you seen God heal someone the doctors said would die? How many times has God intervened and made a way in a situation that seemed impossible? How many times has God provided a job, a special gift, favor with someone who could help, or dozens of other things in a time of need? Have you seen the love of God through a parent who adopts a little battered and bruised war orphan, through a friend who weeps with you in your pain or tries to lift you up in encouragement, or through a stranger that stops to help when your car is stranded along the highway?

Yet, there are times when God does not choose to stop the evil. I do not know why. But, He is God and has a higher plan. He knows all things, the end from the beginning, where our understanding is limited to earthly concepts. God does not go back on His word. When He decided that He did not want a robot for life on earth, but a living, breathing man and woman and gave them freedom of choice, He made a decision that He will not change. God, even though sovereign and wanting to give you His best, will allow you that freedom, whether you make good choices that bring joy and life, or whether you make bad choices that open the door to pain and destruction.

The same thing holds true in regard to our decisions regarding personal salvation. God wants us to want Him! How do you like it when someone is your friend because they want something from you or because they had no other choice? Man expects to earn God's favor and salvation through being good enough or doing enough works to deserve it. If God used this method to grant salvation, it would result in pride, competition and strife, and ultimately it wouldn't work because we are human and can never be good enough in ourselves.

God knew this, and chose to extend grace through faith to the human race as His method to redeem mankind from spiritual death unto eternal life. The crucifixion of Jesus Christ to pay the penalties for sin satisfied God's justice, which was needed because He is a holy God and righteousness had to be fulfilled. Yet, with that true faith in Jesus that saves us, not only do we receive legal "right-standing" with God, but we receive the power of the very life and Spirit of Jesus Christ to enable us to walk according to His good ways… because we want to and not because we are forced to do so, and because we know God's ways are the path that lead to blessing and to the fulfillment of the purposes for which we have been created.

Where we are now, and where we are headed

The troubled times that have come upon this country are not the punishment of God. However, cause and effect is a very real principle at work. We are a people that have largely forsaken the God of our forefathers. Instead, we have chosen to walk in defiance, rebellion, and every manner of sinful lifestyle, allowing the atrocities of murder, crime, violence, immorality, pornography, perversion and insolence to invade our homes and families through every form of media…television, radio, music, and the Internet. The Bible puts it this way:

> *Do not be deceived: God cannot be mocked. A man reaps what he sows. The one who sows to please his sinful nature, from that nature will reap destruction; the one who sows to please the Spirit, from the Spirit will reap eternal life.*

> (Galatians 6:7-8, NIV)

However, I repeat, GOD IS NOT MAD AT AMERICA! He loves America and her people, and desires for every one of them to return to Him. Though as mentioned previously, God allows people to choose—good or bad. It is not His will that anyone should spend eternity in Hell. He desires for all to be saved and be with Him forever.

The Lord does not delay and is not tardy or slow about what He promises, according to some people's conception of slowness, but He is long-suffering (extraordinarily patient) toward you, not desiring that any should perish, but that all should turn to repentance. But the day of the Lord will come like a thief, and then the heavens will vanish (pass away) with a thunderous crash, and the [material] elements [of the universe] will be dissolved with fire, and the earth and the works that are upon it will be burned up.

(2 Peter 3:9-10, AMP)

Do you hear the wake-up call?

Can America survive?

America cannot continue to ignore God and think she can survive. Returning to God is her only hope! In chapter two *Truth or Fiction? Are the Bible's End-Time Prophecies Coming True?*, you will read words that can be very disturbing if you do not have a faith that is anchored in God Almighty, the Creator of heaven and earth.

Dear Reader, if this seems preposterous or unbelievable to you...take a look around. What do you see? Terror? Confusion? Lack? Do not make fun of the living God, or think these words are from the imagination of a silly, Christian fanatic. These are serious times...America cannot survive unless she looks to heaven and asks God for help. But, it cannot be just a few Christians that do this…all Americans must take part. There is hope, and there is help, but God will not reach out His powerful hand to rescue America if we continue to reject Him from the mainstream of our lives.

In the Gospels, there is a story about King Herod, who came to a bitter end. Why? The reason for his destruction is much the same as the reason America has deteriorated and is facing so many challenges now. King Herod received the glory unto himself as if he were God, instead of giving the glory to whom it belongs—to the King of kings and Lord of lords—Jesus Christ, and His Father, the only true living God. This is also a picture of what will bring down the antichrist, whom we will discuss more in-depth a little later.

> *So on a set day Herod, arrayed in royal apparel, sat on his throne and gave an oration to them. And the people kept shouting, "The voice of a god and not of a man!" Then immediately an angel of the Lord struck him, because he did not give glory to God. And he was eaten by worms and died.*
>
> (Acts 12:21-23, NKJV)

It is time to repent and change our direction. It is time to pray, fast, and cry tears of godly sorrow and repentance for our beloved America. Yes, there is hope, and there is help, but it will take a radical change of heart and direction in this country. Politicians cannot do it and the bankers cannot do it; this will need to be a grassroots move of

Americans turning back to their Creator and their true Founder! It is only by a fresh outpouring of God's grace and power through His Holy Spirit that will save America.

> *What sorrow for those who say that evil is good and good is evil, that dark is light and light is dark, that bitter is sweet and sweet is bitter. What sorrow for those who are wise in their own eyes and think themselves so clever.*

(Isaiah 5:20-21, NLT)

My friend, when you pray for our President, Congress and others, be sure to pray for their advisors as well. There are political groups, think tanks, mainstream media, huge corporations and others behind the scenes that influence and manipulate what goes on in this country. There are decisions made behind closed doors that affect you and me, the freedoms we enjoy, and the overall direction taken by those who are visible, the elected officials that we have chosen.

The love of money, greed, and desire for power motivate many decisions and policies. I am not pointing fingers at any one particular person or political agenda, but be aware and if you are a Christian, continue to keep our beloved country—and the world, too—in fervent prayer.

Does this sound like a movie theme in which the bad guys plot to take over the world? This is exactly what the antichrist will do, when he comes into power. Satan, who has always desired to overthrow God and be God himself, will embody this political leader, who most likely will come out of Europe somewhere, and indeed rule over the world. Countries of the world now are already uniting into regions, or unions; i.e. the European Union, the South Asian Union, South American Union, the Pacific Union, the Mediterranean Union and others.

Talks concerning the establishment of a North America Union, comprising the United States, Canada and Mexico, were held behind closed doors during the mid-to-upper first decade of the 2000's. Plans included a NAFTA "Superhighway" that would open up our borders and allow unregulated transport between Mexico City through the U.S. to Central Canada. Part of the Security Prosperity and Partnership organization, the failure of this effort was credited to the work of activist groups who considered this union to be a dangerous threat to American sovereignty. However, in early 2011, American President Barack Obama and Canadian Prime Minister Stephen Harper announced a new security and prosperity initiative between our two countries, in which they plan to initiate a border action plan, which will increase North American security, economic competitiveness, job creation, cooperative trade and travel.

You will find more on the antichrist and his cohort, the false prophet, end-time judgments and other events in chapter two *Truth or Fiction? Are the Bible's End-Time Prophecies Coming True?* How will we recognize the antichrist? Look for a charismatic leader, who will appear to have all the answers. He will come on the global scene, seeming to have the solutions to the world's problems. He will unite the world's economies and currency, and establish a seven-year peace treaty with Israel. He will be well-liked by all the nations, and they will want to unite under him and follow the new world order policies he establishes. But, don't be fooled! The Bible says that when people are saying "peace and security," then war and destruction will come.

This antichrist will control the ability of people to buy and sell by giving them a mark in their forehead or hand. Have you heard about the RFID technology which makes it possible to implant a tiny chip, with all of your personal information and identification, in your body? RFID is also available in tattoo form. It has been developed, tested, approved by the FDA, and is ready for use in humans. This technology is already being used in animals to track them, and has infiltrated into various other components of society, including increasingly, wide-spread use in the retail market to identify and track products. Though a useful inventory procedure at present, this may also, in part, be laying the groundwork for the antichrist's ability to control who can buy and sell. Many believe, and I agree, that this will be the "666" mark talked about in the book of Revelation, which will be used as the dividing line of allegiance between true Christianity and those who willingly choose to follow the antichrist's system.

Beware! Those who take the mark and serve this world ruler, the antichrist, will come not only to earthly destruction, but to eternal damnation. Be forewarned and forearmed with the knowledge of Bible prophecy.

What is the answer?

There is only one answer! There is no alternative. We must repent and turn to God to save us—corporately as a country and each person individually. The message of Jesus is the same today as it was in Bible times:

> *From that time Jesus began to preach and to say, "Repent, for the kingdom of heaven is at hand."*

(Matthew 4:17, NKJV)

Kingdom living

The kingdom of God (or what I call kingdom life, kingdom living or supernatural living) had come because Jesus appeared on the scene. Though born in human form, Jesus was still God, and with Him, He brought a taste of the kingdom of God. Here and now upon the earth, I am referring to the kingdom of God as God's way of doing things, not limited by natural laws or man's earthly understanding.

Beyond the affairs of daily life, lies a glorious afterlife. Those who have received Jesus as Savior and Lord will enter into the fullness of God's kingdom when Jesus returns to earth for them. They will reign forever with their Lord in the new heaven and the new earth. (Read chapter two of this book, as well as the book of Revelation itself for more insight and understanding.)

The Lord delivers from danger and harm

The Apostle Paul knew how to live in intimate, personal relationship with his Lord. Previous to his dramatic conversion, Paul had been the foremost assaulter of the Church. He dragged men and women into prison for their faith and persecuted the Church relentlessly. But, after Paul met Jesus (in a vision that changed his life forever), he not only stopped persecuting the Church, he became the most fervent and prolific preacher out of all the apostles and disciples of Christ. "I am the chiefest of sinners," lamented Paul, as he humbly submitted himself to the call of God to preach. Not many are called to go through as much havoc and trials as Paul suffered for his faith, but even through every imaginable and terrible distress, Paul confidently proclaimed:

> *But you, Timothy, certainly know what I teach, and how I live, and what my purpose in life is. You know my faith, my patience, my love, and my endurance. You know how much persecution and suffering I have endured. You know all about how I was persecuted in Antioch, Iconium, and Lystra—but the Lord rescued me from all of it.*
>
> (2 Timothy 3:10-11, NLT)

Jesus Is coming soon! Are you ready?

Jesus is coming soon! There is no time to waste… no time to think, "I'll do it later." You have no guarantee of tomorrow. Today is the acceptable time of salvation.

35

(Please see the plan of personal salvation in chapter nine *Departing for Heaven at "Gate Jesus": Don't Miss Your Departure Time!* and find out if your eternal future is secure.)

> *And what do you benefit if you gain the whole world but lose your own soul? Is anything worth more than your soul? If anyone is ashamed of me and my message in these adulterous and sinful days, the Son of Man will be ashamed of that person when he returns in the glory of his Father with the holy angels."*

(Mark 8:36-38, NLT)

There is a fearful, tormenting, eternal future for those who reject God, the Creator of all heaven and earth, through denying His Son, Jesus Christ.

My friend, God loves you. He created you for a divine, wonderful purpose and has an exciting, meaningful plan for your life. Even if you have grave sin in your past, or are now walking in unmentionable things, you are precious to the heavenly Father. He has promised to be with you all the days of your life here on earth, if you will receive His Son and allow Him to walk with you.

After this temporary earthly life, things get even better. A place called heaven, where there are no more tears or sorrow, no more sickness or pain, no more lack, strife or struggles, is waiting for you when it's your time to depart from this world. For those who trust in Him and are waiting patiently for His appearing, Jesus promises a heavenly crown.

> *And now the prize awaits me—the crown of*
> *righteousness, which the Lord, the righteous*
> *Judge, will give me on the day of his return.*
> *And the prize is not just for me but for all who*
> *eagerly look forward to his appearing.*
>
> (2 Timothy 4:8, NLT)

Do you hear the wake-up call?

Who Is Expendable?

Population control is already in force in some nations. Whether the motive for population control is the need to ration food because there is not enough for everybody, or because certain segments of the population are seen as not valuable, it is a dreadful and dangerous thing for man to play God and choose who should live and who should die. The determination of "quality of life" is weighed against "right to live," and becomes the qualifying factor for whether a person should continue to live or would be better off dead.

Have we come to a point in America's history where human life is so devalued that some people are considered not necessary, unprofitable, unproductive, or unfit for society? In other words, they are considered "expendable."

I pray this will never happen to America, but consider the following groups. Will they one day be labeled "expendable" and legal extermination become a reality?

The sick –

The hospitals are filled with the sick and dying. Because of costs involved, maybe shortage of medical staff, and because life is not seen as sacred as God sees it, decisions of whether to take patients off life support—or not even put them on it in the first place—are being increasingly left up to family members whose inexperience, lack of knowledge, and sometimes emotional instabilities or even grievances against the sick person may cloud their abilities to make good decisions. The patient's or family's lack of insurance or ability to pay for rising medical costs may affect the quality of treatment the patient receives. National Health Insurance is seen as the solution, but in reality, it opens the way for a welfare mentality, long delays and waiting for services, sometimes an inferior standard of care, and an increased tax burden on citizens.

The aged –

Euthanasia is practiced in some countries, where it is reasoned that those who are aged have lived full lives upon the earth. There is not enough food and room for everybody; therefore, it's time to make room for the young, strong, and those who are in their prime of life. It is better that the aged are sacrificed than for the youthful members of society to go without. In the past in America, there was a notorious doctor who accommodated the death wishes of people who wanted to put an end to their suffering. Will this become the status-quo for senior citizens over a certain pre-determined age?

Street people and welfare recipients –

Often seen as not contributing to society and as a tax burden, will these people someday be seen as "expendable?" Today in the midst of financial crisis, due to company layoffs and debts too big to handle, some families are taking to the streets or have become dependant on welfare checks because they have no other choice. They are hard workers, but jobs have become scarce and are not always available.

Mentally retarded –

These too are deemed not suited for society, often considered unproductive, and in an uncertain future, perhaps a drain on limited food supplies and other commodities. They are seen as not contributing to the mainstream of life in a positive way, and their care and "maintenance" too expensive to continue. In many cases, I believe spiritual help and taking some off anti-depressants and other medicines and treatments, the results of which are sometimes worse than their benefits, would yield surprisingly sane and productive citizens.

Unborn babies –

The question of pro-choice or pro-life has been a political and social hotspot for many years and the practice of abortion is already occurring in this country. Whether a moral issue, a "choice" issue for parents, or a shortage of food issue, the extermination of unborn babies is likely not only to continue, but to increase as times become more difficult.

Christians –

There is a rising movement in other religious groups and non-religious groups to rid the world of Christians, who are labeled as "intolerant" and guilty of "hate crimes." Also, those who study what the Bible has to say about the times we are living in and the times to come (see especially Matthew 24, Revelation, and Old Testament books like Daniel and Ezekiel) blame the "God of the Christians and Jews" for the horrors that are happening—and are soon to increase in intensity upon the earth. These groups and individuals believe the only way to solve these serious challenges now facing the world is to get rid of the Christians and their God. Some will even believe that they can fight against Jesus Christ Himself (Please see more about this in chapter two: *Truth or Fiction? Are the Bible's End-Time Prophecies Coming True?*.)

and Jews –

The Jews have long been a target of anti-Semitism. The Middle East's desire to destroy Israel extends beyond the borders of this tiny country, to all who would stand in support of her, even to America, as of this writing. Yet, it is imperative for America to remain a friend to Israel.

Do you know that God loves all people—the Jews, the Arabs and other Gentiles, and the Christians? All are precious in His sight. With God all things are possible! When a country is ruled by Him there is prosperity and no need to choose between life and death. In God's eyes, all men, women, boys and girls, including unborn babies, have value; unlike the world's view of human worth. The

God of heaven and earth can, and will, provide for the needs when a person's or nation's trust is turned to Him.

Is America losing her freedoms?

"Two hundred years ago the United States Constitution was written as a guide for America's unique experiment in freedom. Today, the free society that the Founders envisaged is barely identifiable," says Texas Congressman Ron Paul. Paul, who is a current contender for the Republican Party presidential candidate nomination, is still saying the same thing today, 25 years later.

(Source: Freedom Under Siege, by Ron Paul, p. 1 Dec 31, 1987)

Are we really spying out terrorists, or are Americans losing their freedoms? In every major city, and then some, "red light" cameras can be seen on street corners. Added to this, there are other cameras strung on street poles or mounted in portable tower-like structures that focus in every direction, click-click-clicking their photos. It is said that satellites situated way above in the sky can see into a person's house and apparatuses now located in planes that fly overhead can zoom in on a person's facial features.

Prison camps, with an unofficial average estimate of several hundred locations, exist in America today. Some of these are said to be warehouses that have armed guards and a "no entry" space surrounding them for civilians as well as restricted air space above. Are these all for terrorists, or is someone expecting a revolution?

The threat of nuclear bomb attacks has intensified as America becomes increasingly unpopular, the result of her unsolicited positioning of troops throughout the world. However, it is hopeful that the new administration will bring an improved outlook to the world that will restore respect toward America, and she will regain her long-honored reputation of being a peacemaker, rather than a warmongering influence in the world.

At the writing of this book, the European Union is experiencing a "euro crisis." Greece, Italy, Portugal and Spain have already accepted billions in bailouts from the EU to help rescue their failing economies. The Federal Reserve has stated that the "euro crisis poses a significant threat to the U.S." Financial experts believe the U.S. dollar will follow suit after an anticipated crash of the euro currency.

Couple this with our government's history of printing more money and further devaluing the dollar in order to "bailout" major corporations, banks, and the mortgage and credit industries, we are a nation headed for disaster! Bailouts are not the answer. They lead only to a corporate welfare mentality. One corporation is bailed out, then others will line up after it, and corporation after corporation will fall. Those who survive will consolidate and become a monopoly, causing further stock market crashes and rising prices.

I am an American and I love my country. I share these things with the desire of alerting people to become aware and take notice that indeed the events that are happening today in the United States of America and around the world are setting the scene for the fulfillment of Bible prophecy—God's plan for these end times of the world as we know it. (Please see more about this in chapter two: *Truth or Fiction? Are the Bible's End-Time Prophecies Coming True?*.)

But, there is hope!
America has yet to see her finest hour…

I believe that despite all the problems and threats looming on America's horizon, that we are a people who will rise to the occasion and, with God's mercy and help, America will be restored to her greatness once again. (See more in chapter three: *America's Finest Hour: A People of Faith and Courage Arise!)*

> *Don't you see how wonderfully kind, tolerant, and patient God is with you? Does this mean nothing to you? Can't you see that his kindness is intended to turn you from your sin? But because you are stubborn and refuse to turn from your sin, you are storing up terrible punishment for yourself. For a day of anger is coming, when God's righteous judgment will be revealed.*
>
> (Romans 2:3-5, NLT)

It is possible for God's goodness and mercy to override His righteous judgment that is prophesied in the Scripture we just read. God loves the American people, just as He loves all people, and desires to bless this country. From the years since its discovery…to the founding fathers, the pilgrims, the pioneers to the present new millennium…

America has been a nation of prosperity and honor. Through the decades as God has been removed from public life—government, schools, media and entertainment—and replaced with the idols of self, greed, violence, and perversion of everything good, our land of plenty has deteriorated to its current condition.

If America chooses not to turn to her Creator…if you and I choose not to return to the God who loves us, then we will have no one—not God, not others—to blame, but only to look to our own poor choices and decisions.

In the coming days in America, and around the world, everything that can be shaken will be shaken! Those things that are built upon the "solid rock," which is Jesus Christ, will alone remain standing. Friend, if you have not already done so, I urge you to ask Jesus to take control of your life and your future, and He will develop in you an unshakeable faith that will carry you through whatever lies ahead to certain victory!

Chapter Two

Truth or Fiction?
Are the Bible's End-Time Prophecies Coming True?

This chapter will share portions of the book of Revelation, the closing book of the Bible, that so many people are talking about today. People everywhere are asking, "Are the Bible's end-time prophecies coming true?"

Yes, my friend, they are… and with rapidly approaching speed and clarity!

If you are a student of Bible prophecy, as you turn on the evening news, you will scc it unfolding right before your very eyes. There is not enough space in this chapter to cover the entire book of Revelation, but as we go through, we will hit upon some of the most relevant chapters relating to current events today and those soon to come.

Receive a special blessing!

Be sure to get out your Bible and read the entire book of Revelation. Ask God to give you wisdom and understanding as you read it. God promises a special blessing to those who read, hear and act in accordance with the words that are written in the book of Revelation.

Blessed is the one who reads the words of this prophecy, and blessed are those who hear it and take to heart what is written in it, because the time is near.

(Revelation 1:3, NIV)

The book of Revelation is the revelation of Jesus Christ and the things that were, are, and are yet to come upon planet earth. The revelation was given to the Apostle John who has written down these things to inform and encourage Christians and to warn all who will listen that the kingdom of God is at hand!

Chapter 1 of Revelation shows the glory of Jesus, the One who shed His blood for the restoration of mankind's relationship with their Creator, God, and the Father of all.

8 "I am the Alpha and the Omega—the beginning and the end," says the Lord God. "I am the one who is, who always was, and who is still to come—the Almighty One."

9 I, John, am your brother and your partner in suffering and in God's Kingdom and in the patient endurance to which Jesus calls

46

*us. I was exiled to the island of Patmos
for preaching the word of God and for my
testimony about Jesus.*

*10 It was the Lord's Day, and I was
worshiping in the Spirit. Suddenly, I heard
behind me a loud voice like a trumpet blast.*

*11 It said, "Write in a book everything you
see, and send it to the seven churches in
the cities of Ephesus, Smyrna, Pergamum,
Thyatira, Sardis, Philadelphia, and
Laodicea."*

(Revelation 1:8-11, NLT)

When John saw Jesus in the heavenly vision, he was astonished. But Jesus reassured him:

*When I (John) saw (Jesus), I fell at his feet as
if I were dead. But he laid his right hand on
me and said, "Don't be afraid! I am the First
and the Last. I am the living one. I died, but
look—I am alive forever and ever! And I hold
the keys of death and the grave.*

(Revelation 1: 17-18 NLT)

Jesus, our Lord and soon-coming King is alive! Moreover, He holds the keys of death and the grave. This means that the Christian will never be conquered by death, but will have victory over the grave when Jesus comes to receive His faithful ones unto Himself. Christian friend, no matter what you face in life on the earth, it is but a short time until you see the face of your Savior and live forever with Him—with no more tears, pain, problems or earthly limitations. You will receive an incorruptible body that will never get sick or hold you back any more (1 Corinthians 15:53-54).

Jesus' message to the seven churches

In chapter 2 and 3, Jesus gives a message to the seven churches. This has a two-fold meaning. The churches represent seven church ages in history since the Church began, culminating in the last two churches Philadelphia and Laodicea that co-exist today. Philadelphia is a picture of the true church, following Christ, witnessing and being ready for His second coming. Laodicea, on the other hand, is a church that is fat with the riches of materialism and a complacency that is more focused on the things of this world than the things of God that are the true riches.

The second meaning represented by the seven churches shows a composite of many of the weaknesses that exist in the Church today. In each church, Christ commended the believers for their strengths, for what they were doing right. But, He also issued a strong warning to every church but Philadelphia. Jesus sternly pointed out to them their area of weakness, whether compromise, greed, immorality, doctrinal error, or a host of other faults, with a serious warning about what and how they needed to change if they were going to "endure until the end" and receive eternal life in the kingdom of heaven.

Jesus began and ended his message with a word of wisdom to them—and to us, the Church today:

*"Anyone with ears to hear must listen to the
Spirit and understand what he is saying to the
churches."*

(Revelation 2:22, NLT)

I have not detailed the specific message to each church in
this chapter, because you will find an expanded description
when you get to chapter five *Destruction from Within the
Church: Differences, Divisions, and Divine Direction.*

The Rapture of the Church

Chapter 4 begins with John peering into heaven and
being invited to "Come up here."

Some Bible teachers believe this phrase is not meant
solely to one person, John, but to all believers and that it
is the place which pinpoints the time of the Rapture of the
Church.

*Then as I looked, I saw a door standing open
in heaven, and the same voice I had heard
before spoke to me like a trumpet blast. The
voice said, "Come up here, and I will show
you what must happen after this.*

(Revelation 4:1, NLT)

Others believe that later references in Revelation show
a sea of innumerable believers worshiping the Lamb, and
that this comes before the judgments of God are poured out,
indicating that the Rapture occurs, taking the Church out
of the earth, before the time of the tribulation that is to try
mankind. Still others believe that believers will go through

the first three and one half years of this tribulation period and then be caught up with Christ in the air (raptured) or that believers will have to endure the entire tribulation period of seven years. These are called pre-trib, mid-trib and post-trib theories.

You will have to decide for yourself, with the help of the Holy Spirit, which is the Spirit of Christ, as you pray and read the Word of God. I am with the pre-tribulation crowd and believe there are other Scriptures in the Bible that indicate that those who have been born again prior to the time of tribulation—both dead and alive—will escape the time of tribulation. The Rapture itself is described in 1 Thessalonians, chapter 4:

> *13 And now, dear brothers and sisters, we want you to know what will happen to the believers who have died so you will not grieve like people who have no hope.*
>
> *14 For since we believe that Jesus died and was raised to life again, we also believe that when Jesus returns, God will bring back with him the believers who have died.*
>
> *15 We tell you this directly from the Lord: We who are still living when the Lord returns will not meet him ahead of those who have died.*
>
> *16 For the Lord himself will come down from heaven with a commanding shout, with the voice of the archangel, and with the trumpet call of God. First, the Christians who have died will rise from their graves.*

17 Then, together with them, we who are still alive and remain on the earth will be caught up in the clouds to meet the Lord in the air. Then we will be with the Lord forever.

18 So encourage each other with these words.

(1 Thessalonians 4:13-18, NLT)

And then again in 1 Corinthians, chapter 15, where the Apostle Paul shares for the benefit of believers of all ages a revelation He received concerning the "mystery" commonly called the "Rapture."

51 But let me reveal to you a wonderful secret. We will not all die, but we will all be transformed! It will happen

52 in a moment, in the blink of an eye, when the last trumpet is blown. For when the trumpet sounds, those who have died will be raised to live forever. And we who are living will also be transformed.

53 For our dying bodies must be transformed into bodies that will never die; our mortal bodies must be transformed into immortal bodies.

54 Then, when our dying bodies have been transformed into bodies that will never die, this Scripture will be fulfilled: "Death is swallowed up in victory.

55 O death, where is your victory? O death, where is your sting?"

(1 Corinthians 15:51-55, NLT)

Further, in chapter 4, a great worship scene in heaven is vividly described, which includes twenty-four elders sitting on twenty-four thrones surrounding the throne of the Most High God. These are the twelve patriarchs from the Old Testament and the twelve apostles from the New Testament, representative of all humanity from the beginning of God's creation of mankind. Also, surrounding the throne are four living beings described like this:

> *The first of these living beings was like a lion; the second was like an ox; the third had a human face; and the fourth was like an eagle in flight. Each of these living beings had six wings, and their wings were covered all over with eyes, inside and out.*

(Revelation 4:7-8, NLT)

Later in chapter 5, angels are added to the glorious worship—thousands, even millions of angels. At this time, a heavenly scroll is introduced, but it is sealed with seven seals. A search begins throughout heaven to find someone who is worthy to open the scroll. Finally, the Lamb of God (Jesus Christ) steps forward. Yes, He alone is worthy to open the heavenly scroll which contains the plans of God which are shortly to come to pass upon the earth. The worship continues, as the One, who redeemed the souls of men with His own blood, breaks the seals, one-by-one, and opens the scroll.

Notice the similarities between Matthew 24 quoted in chapter one of this book with the following Revelation chapters 6 and 7, which describe the horrors that happen on earth at the opening of each of the first six of the seven seals. Jesus first told of these things that are coming upon the earth in Matthew 24, and now again he shows a vision of them to John in the book of Revelation. This is a double witness, which indicates the reality, urgency, and intensity, not only of the things to come, but of Jesus' warning to us to be ready and to share the Gospel with others so that they are ready, too!

The antichrist is revealed, signaling the beginning of the tribulation period:

As I watched, the Lamb broke the first of the seven seals on the scroll. Then I heard one of the four living beings say with a voice like thunder, "Come!" I looked up and saw a white horse standing there. Its rider carried a bow, and a crown was placed on his head. He rode out to win many battles and gain the victory.

(Revelation 6:1-2, NLT)

War and violence broke out:

When the Lamb broke the second seal, I heard the second living being say, "Come!" Then another horse appeared, a red one. Its rider was given a mighty sword and the authority to take peace from the earth. And there was war and slaughter everywhere.

(Revelation 6:3-4, NLT)

Famine covered the earth:

*When the Lamb broke the third seal, I heard
the third living being say, "Come!" I looked
up and saw a black horse, and its rider was
holding a pair of scales in his hand. And I
heard a voice from among the four living
beings say, "A loaf of wheat bread or three
loaves of barley will cost a day's pay. And
don't waste the olive oil and wine."*

(Revelation 6:5-6, NLT)

Death ravages one-quarter of the earth:

*When the Lamb broke the fourth seal, I heard
the fourth living being say, "Come!" I looked
up and saw a horse whose color was pale
green. Its rider was named Death, and his
companion was the Grave. These two were
given authority over one-fourth of the earth,
to kill with the sword and famine and disease
and wild animals.*

(Revelation 6:7-8, NLT)

The martyrs of Christ revealed:

*When the Lamb broke the fifth seal, I saw
under the altar the souls of all who had been
martyred for the word of God and for being
faithful in their testimony.*

(Revelation 6:9, NLT)

The day of God's wrath:

12 I watched as the Lamb broke the sixth seal, and there was a great earthquake. The sun became as dark as black cloth, and the moon became as red as blood.

13 Then the stars of the sky fell to the earth like green figs falling from a tree shaken by a strong wind.

14 The sky was rolled up like a scroll, and all of the mountains and islands were moved from their places.

15 Then everyone—the kings of the earth, the rulers, the generals, the wealthy, the powerful, and every slave and free person—all hid themselves in the caves and among the rocks of the mountains.

16 And they cried to the mountains and the rocks, "Fall on us and hide us from the face of the one who sits on the throne and from the wrath of the Lamb.

17 For the great day of their wrath has come, and who is able to survive?"

(Revelation 6:12-17, NLT)

God's People Will Be Preserved

1 Then I saw four angels standing at the four corners of the earth, holding back the four winds so they did not blow on the earth or the sea, or even on any tree.

2 And I saw another angel coming up from the east, carrying the seal of the living God. And he shouted to those four angels, who had been given power to harm land and sea,

3 "Wait! Don't harm the land or the sea or the trees until we have placed the seal of God on the foreheads of his servants."

4 And I heard how many were marked with the seal of God—144,000 were sealed from all the tribes of Israel.

9 After this I saw a vast crowd, too great to count, from every nation and tribe and people and language, standing in front of the throne and before the Lamb. They were clothed in white robes and held palm branches in their hands.

10 And they were shouting with a mighty shout, "Salvation comes from our God who sits on the throne and from the Lamb!"

(Revelation 7:1-4, 9-10 NLT)

God will take care of you!

In the previously quoted Scripture about famine covering the earth (Revelation 6:5-6, note the last seven words, *"And don't waste the olive oil and wine."* In the New King James Version, it says, *"Hurt not the oil and the wine."* Dr. Morris Cerullo, worldwide evangelist and president of Morris Cerullo World Evangelism says, "This refers to God's blood-bought (wine) and spirit-filled (oil) people. Similarly in the Old Testament, when the death angel passed over Egypt in the final plague before Pharaoh let the people of Israel go; the people of God were protected when they smeared blood on their doorposts. That blood, symbolic of the redeeming blood shed by Jesus Christ for our salvation, protected the people of God from the judgments that were going on all around them. Do you belong to Christ? Then, you are the "people of God," and you will have the same protection in these latter days. You do not need to fear; God will take care of you and your household just as He did for the Israelites in Egypt."

The opening of the seventh seal

Revelation, chapter 8 brings the opening of the final seventh seal, which begins the seven trumpet blasts, continuing the wrath of God upon the earth during the dreaded tribulation period.

The Lamb Breaks the Seventh Seal

When the Lamb broke the seventh seal on the scroll, there was silence throughout heaven for about half an hour. I saw the seven angels who stand before God, and they were given seven trumpets.

(Revelation 8:1-2, NLT)

In chapters 8 and 9, the first six of seven angels sound their mighty trumpet blasts as the wrath of God upon the earth continued.

The first trumpet:

The first angel blew his trumpet, and hail and fire mixed with blood were thrown down on the earth. One-third of the earth was set on fire, one-third of the trees were burned, and all the green grass was burned.

(Revelation 8:7, NLT)

The second trumpet:

Then the second angel blew his trumpet, and a great mountain of fire was thrown into the sea. One-third of the water in the sea became blood, one-third of all things living in the sea died, and one-third of all the ships on the sea were destroyed.

(Revelation 8:8-9, NLT)

The third trumpet:

Then the third angel blew his trumpet, and a great star fell from the sky, burning like a torch. It fell on one-third of the rivers and on the springs of water. The name of the star was Bitterness. It made one-third of the water bitter, and many people died from drinking the bitter water.

(Revelation 8:10-11, NLT)

The fourth trumpet:

Then the fourth angel blew his trumpet, and one-third of the sun was struck, and one-third

of the moon, and one-third of the stars, and
they became dark. And one-third of the day
was dark, and also one-third of the night.
Then I looked, and I heard a single eagle
crying loudly as it flew through the air,
"Terror, terror, terror to all who belong to this
world because of what will happen when the
last three angels blow their trumpets."

(Revelation 8:12-13, NLT)

The fifth trumpet:

(The fifth trumpet brings the first terror)
Then the fifth angel blew his trumpet, and I
saw a star that had fallen to earth from the
sky, and he was given the key to the shaft of
the bottomless pit. When he opened it, smoke
poured out as though from a huge furnace,
and the sunlight and air turned dark from the
smoke. Then locusts came from the smoke and
descended on the earth, and they were given
power to sting like scorpions...

(Revelation 9:1-3, NLT)

The sixth trumpet

(The sixth trumpet brings the second terror)

13 Then the sixth angel blew his trumpet...

15 then the four angels who had been
prepared for this hour and day and month and
year were turned loose to kill one-third of all
the people on earth.

> *16 I heard the size of their army, which was*
> *200 million mounted troops...*
>
> *18 One-third of all the people on earth were*
> *killed by these three plagues—by the fire and*
> *smoke and burning sulfur that came from the*
> *mouths of the horses...*
>
> *20 But the people who did not die in these*
> *plagues still refused to repent of their evil*
> *deeds and turn to God...*
>
> (Revelation 9:13, 15-16, 18, 20, NLT)

In chapter 10, an angel announces that there will be no delay and when the seventh angel blows his trumpet, God's mysterious plan will be fulfilled. But, before we hear about the seventh trumpet, chapter 11 tells about two mysterious witnesses. Some people think that these are Moses and Elijah because during the life of Christ, they met with Him on the Mount of Transfiguration (Matthew 17:3). Others think these two witnesses will be Elijah and Enoch because the Scripture says that it is appointed men once to die (Hebrews 9:27) and these two men were taken by God and did not die an earthly death.

These two witnesses are sent to earth during the tribulation to preach the Gospel and prophesy. Initially, no one can harm them. If anyone tries to harm these two prophets, fire flashes from their mouths and consumes their enemies. However, after they finish their testimony, the beast (more about this in Revelation 17 and 18) puts them to death and their bodies lay slain in the streets. The world gloats over their death, until three and a half days later, God breathes life into them and brings them back to heaven. Seeing this, the world becomes terrified.

> **The seventh trumpet:**
> *(The seventh trumpet brings the third terror)*
> *Then, in heaven, the Temple of God was*
> *opened and the Ark of his covenant could be*
> *seen inside the Temple. Lightning flashed,*
> *thunder crashed and roared, and there was an*
> *earthquake and a terrible hailstorm.*
>
> (Revelation 11:19, NLT)

Satan could not kill our Redeemer!

In chapter 12, there are basically two scenes. The players in the first scene are a woman in great pain, who is about to give birth to a man-child. Standing in front of her is a large red dragon with seven heads and ten horns ready to devour the baby as soon as it is born.

> *She gave birth to a son who was to rule all*
> *nations with an iron rod. And her child was*
> *snatched away from the dragon and was*
> *caught up to God and to his throne. And the*
> *woman fled into the wilderness, where God*
> *had prepared a place to care for her for 1,260*
> *days.*
>
> (Revelation 12:5-6, NLT)

This is a picture of Jesus Christ, who was birthed out of the womb of the virgin Mary. (Many believe the woman is symbolic of Israel, out of which Christ came in a natural sense.) The dragon, or satan, tried to kill Jesus before He was "born," and then again while He was living on the earth so that He could not fulfill His assignment from God to redeem mankind. But, it didn't work! Christ came to earth, was crucified and rose again! Jesus remains in heaven at the right side of His Father until the time He will descend from heaven in the clouds to call up His saints (His followers, those who have had a born-again experience and have the Holy Spirit of God dwelling inside of them.)

We should note too, that the Scripture above shows that God cares for His people now and during the great tribulation. If Jesus is your personal Savior, and for the Jews—their long-awaited Messiah—be at peace. God will take care of you. And, dear friend, if this is not true at this moment, you can become born again simply by asking Jesus to come into your life. If you mean it with your heart, pray something like this:

>*"Dear God,*
>
>*I believe Jesus is Your Son and was crucified for my sins so that I could be forgiven and have a personal relationship with You. I believe Jesus rose again to life and is in heaven with You now, and just as He, someday, I too will live with You for eternity. I repent of my sins and right now, this moment, I ask Jesus to come into my heart and take charge of my life. I am now and forever a born-again child of God! Amen."*

You can read more about this wonderful experience into which you have just entered in chapter nine *Departing for Heaven at "Gate Jesus": Don't Miss Your Departure Time!*

The war between Satan and God's angels in the heavenlies

The other magnificent scene in chapter 12 is a war that breaks out in heaven. You didn't think there could be war in heaven, did you?

> *Then there was war in heaven. Michael and his angels fought against the dragon and his angels. And the dragon lost the battle, and he and his angels were forced out of heaven.*
>
> (Revelation 12:7-8, NLT)

Praise God—the good side wins! Satan is defeated and tossed out of heaven. The bad side to this is that he is thrown down to earth and pursues God's people. But once again, do not fear as mentioned above, because God has prepared a place, a way and a promise to care for you. The following Scripture is a great promise that we will overcome satan once and for all. The context of it refers to the saints that are in heaven, but this is an incredible principle for us as born-again believers to use in our "spiritual warfare" here and now upon the earth.

> *And they have defeated him by the blood of the Lamb and by their testimony. And they*

did not love their lives so much that they were
afraid to die.

(Revelation 12:11, NLT)

So, my dear brother and sister in Christ, you cannot lose. God will take good care of you on the earth. Even if you die, for your faith in Jesus or from a natural cause, there is no fear. God will give you grace and it is but a short moment from the time you leave your earthly body until you are in His glorious presence in heaven! Death is a subject most of us do not like to think about, but for the Christian it is the departure from the pains and limitations of earthly existence to our glorious, eternal inheritance that God has prepared for those who accept His invitation to salvation through His Son, Jesus Christ.

For I fully expect and hope that I will never
be ashamed, but that I will continue to be bold
for Christ, as I have been in the past. And I
trust that my life will bring honor to Christ,
whether I live or die. For to me, living means
living for Christ, and dying is even better. But
if I live, I can do more fruitful work for Christ.
So I really don't know which is better.

(Philippians 1:20-22, NLT)

54 When they heard this, they were furious
and gnashed their teeth at him.

55 But Stephen, full of the Holy Spirit, looked
up to heaven and saw the glory of God, and
Jesus standing at the right hand of God.

56 "Look," he said, "I see heaven open and the Son of Man standing at the right hand of God."

57 At this they covered their ears and, yelling at the top of their voices, they all rushed at him,

58 dragged him out of the city and began to stone him. Meanwhile, the witnesses laid their clothes at the feet of a young man named Saul.

59 While they were stoning him, Stephen prayed, "Lord Jesus, receive my spirit."

60 Then he fell on his knees and cried out, "Lord, do not hold this sin against them." When he had said this, he fell asleep.

(Acts 7:54-60, NIV)

Stephen, like Christ, asked forgiveness for his tormentors and gave up his spirit unto (earthly) death. I personally believe when he saw the glory of God, his focus was so surely fixed on God's glory that he probably didn't even notice any pain he suffered. The reward is far greater and not to be compared with any momentary pain a Christian might endure.

Will we have a new world order?

In chapter 13, we read about not one, but two world leaders—a world government leader and a world church leader. Unlike the current condition in America of separation of church and state, the coming global government will be joined together with the world church, at least for a season.

As mentioned in chapter one of this book, the signs are all around us. For decades various political leaders, financial leaders and others have talked secretly behind closed doors about a new world order, but news is starting to leak out more and more in recent years. The solution for the twin issues of seeking peace and economic recovery will increasingly point to nations joining together under a global political and economic leadership. Some call it a "one-world government;" others use the term "new world order." On the surface, it sounds good. What could be better than the world working together in harmony? The problem is however, that this will not be a true peace...nor true economic prosperity. Both will fail as we will see a little later in this book.

We see a beast rising out of the sea described as having seven heads and ten horns. The Bible says something very interesting about this beast:

> *I saw that one of the heads of the beast seemed wounded beyond recovery—but the fatal wound was healed! The whole world marveled at this miracle and gave allegiance to the beast.*

> (Revelation 13:3, NLT)

This beast, whom we'll talk about more in depth in chapters 17 and 18, is killed, but just like Christ, he rises again to life (on the earth; he does not ascend to heaven). This causes many people to be fooled into thinking that the beast—this world government leader—must be God. And indeed, he will call himself, "God."

The infamous "666" mark of the beast

Another world leader becomes prominent, who is the world church leader. They work together. The world leader desires that all religions become one, and worship him. The world religious leader will convince people to make an "image" of this beast, which will both speak and cause all people—rich and poor, small and great, slave and free—to receive a mark on their forehead or their hand which will allow them to buy and sell. Can you see this coming, my friend? Our current credit and debit cards will someday become obsolete and replaced by a small RFID micro chip, like a minute computer containing all your personal information, that will be inserted in the body. Technology is already available that allows scans of the eyes and hands to be read. This would certainly fit the description of an identifying mark in the forehead or hand.

But those who belong to Jesus Christ will not receive this mark; they will be persecuted, and many will die for their faith. Most Bible scholars believe that the Church of true believers in Jesus Christ will have already been raptured to heaven, and that these who are left upon the earth are those who will become Christians during the time of the great tribulation. So my friend, if you have not received Christ as your Savior and Lord, do so now, so that you can go with Christ in the Rapture and not have to remain and suffer at the hand of the antichrist. (See more about this in chapter nine *Departing for Heaven at "Gate Jesus": Don't Miss Your Departure Time!)*

Warnings of three angels

Chapter 14 opens up with the saints of all ages represented by, but not limited to, the 144,000 who have remained pure and true to Christ, and now are worshiping Him with a new song that only those who know Christ can sing—the song of the redeemed.

In this chapter also, the apostle John sees in a vision three angels who fly by, each giving a warning to the people of the earth. The first angel proclaims God's word to the world and gives them a final opportunity to repent and be saved for eternity. This angel says:

> *"Fear God," he shouted. "Give glory to him.*
> *For the time has come when he will sit as*
> *judge. Worship him who made the heavens, the*
> *earth, the sea, and all the springs of water."*
>
> (Revelation 14:7, NLT)

The second angel announces the coming fall of "Babylon," which is symbolic here of the apostate church that will come to its demise. Babylon also represents the "world system." We will see more about this event in chapters 17-19.

The third angel warns people about the coming destruction for those who are deceived and make the decision to worship the antichrist, taking his mark in themselves.

> *Then a third angel followed them, shouting,*
> *"Anyone who worships the beast and his*
> *statue or who accepts his mark on the*
> *forehead or on the hand must drink the*

wine of God's anger. It has been poured full strength into God's cup of wrath. And they will be tormented with fire and burning sulfur in the presence of the holy angels and the Lamb. The smoke of their torment will rise forever and ever, and they will have no relief day or night, for they have worshiped the beast and his statue and have accepted the mark of his name."

(Revelation 14:9-11, NLT)

I sincerely urge you to be among those who worship the one true God of heaven and earth and do not be fooled by the god of this world. The consequences are too terrible and they last forever. God is God! His ways are higher than our ways, and there are some things we will never understand until we get to heaven. But, God is a loving God and He does not desire that anyone should follow the devil and his angels into a place of everlasting torment.

The Lord does not delay and is not tardy or slow about what He promises, according to some people's conception of slowness, but He is long-suffering (extraordinarily patient) toward you, not desiring that any should perish, but that all should turn to repentance. But the day of the Lord will come like a thief, and then the heavens will vanish (pass away) with a thunderous crash, and the [material] elements [of the universe] will be dissolved with fire, and the earth and the works that are upon it will be burned up.

(2 Peter 3:8-10, AMP)

Victory and destruction

Chapter 15 opens up with a scene of both victory and destruction. Victory for the people of God who have overcome and destruction for the inhabitants of earth who have rejected God.

> *Then I* (John) *saw in heaven another marvelous event of great significance. Seven angels were holding the seven last plagues, which would bring God's wrath to completion. I saw before me what seemed to be a glass sea mixed with fire. And on it stood all the people who had been victorious over the beast and his statue and the number representing his name...*
>
> (Revelation 15:1-2, NLT)

The seven bowl plagues are poured out upon the earth

Chapter 16 describes the seven last plagues, some of which you'll notice repeat the previous seal and trumpet judgments, but now are unleashed to a greater degree of intensity. These are called "vial" or "bowl" plagues and will be poured out one-by-one on the earth.

The first angel:

So the first angel left the Temple and poured out his bowl on the earth, and horrible, malignant sores broke out on everyone who had the mark of the beast and who worshiped his statue.

(Revelation 16:2, NLT)

The second angel:

Then the second angel poured out his bowl on the sea, and it became like the blood of a corpse. And everything in the sea died.

(Revelation 16:3, NLT)

The third angel:

Then the third angel poured out his bowl on the rivers and springs, and they became blood...

(Revelation 16:4, NLT)

The fourth angel:

Then the fourth angel poured out his bowl on the sun, causing it to scorch everyone with its fire.

(Revelation 16:8, NLT)

The fifth angel:

Then the fifth angel poured out his bowl on the throne of the beast, and his kingdom was plunged into darkness. His subjects ground their teeth in anguish...

(Revelation 16:10, NLT)

This bowl (or vial) judgment is poured out on the beast, the antichrist who is the world leader, and plunges his kingdom into darkness. The people of the world who worshiped the beast will be filled with sorrow and terror.

The sixth angel:

Then the sixth angel poured out his bowl on the great Euphrates River, and it dried up so that the kings from the east could march their armies toward the west without hindrance.

(Revelation 16:12, NLT)

The battle of Armageddon

This is where the famed battle of Armageddon comes in. A series of three battles erupt against Israel. Russia, along with probably Egypt and some Arab nations, make the first attack. Then China, and possibly other nations from the Orient, come from the east to join Russia for the second battle. Finally, all nations gather together to come against Israel to destroy her. It is at this point where Jesus Himself steps in and defends Israel and all the nations are defeated. Be ready! The time of Jesus' second coming is at hand. Here, Jesus says:

"Look, I will come as unexpectedly as a thief! Blessed are all who are watching for me, who keep their clothing ready so they will not have to walk around naked and ashamed."

(Revelation 16:15, NLT)

The seventh angel:

Then the seventh angel poured out his bowl into the air. And a mighty shout came from the throne in the Temple, saying, "It is finished!"

(Revelation 16:17, NLT)

Thunder, lightening and the greatest earthquake in history devastates the earth along with 100 pound hailstones falling from heaven!

There is much more detail concerning the seven plagues listed above in chapter 16. Please be sure to read the entire chapter, and the entire book of Revelation, because so much of it is left out in the limited space available in this book. What do you think happened on the earth after each plague was poured out? The people groaned and cursed the Name of God and of His Christ, and did not repent of their wickedness and unbelief.

The great harlot and the beast

Chapter 17 expands upon what we learned in chapter 13 about the uniting of the one-world government leader with the religious leader, who identifies with Christianity because he is described as having two horns (symbolic of the horns of a lamb, one of the Names of Christ—the Lamb of God) but who is demonically controlled because the Scripture says he spoke as a "dragon," one of the names attributed to satan in the Bible.

> *3 So the angel took me in the Spirit into the wilderness. There I saw a woman sitting on a scarlet beast that had seven heads and ten horns, and blasphemies against God were written all over it.*
>
> *4 The woman wore purple and scarlet clothing and beautiful jewelry made of gold and precious gems and pearls. In her hand she*

held a gold goblet full of obscenities and the impurities of her immorality.

5 A mysterious name was written on her forehead: "Babylon the Great, Mother of All Prostitutes and Obscenities in the World."

6 I could see that she was drunk—drunk with the blood of God's holy people who were witnesses for Jesus...

9 "This calls for a mind with understanding: The seven heads of the beast represent the seven hills where the woman rules. They also represent seven kings.

(Revelation 17:3-6, 9 NLT)

The woman represents the apostate church of today. This includes many that are in the Laodicean church described earlier and is the church that commits spiritual adultery with the world. There is a strong move today for religions to unite together—some Christians, Muslims and others—as the world readies itself for the appearance of the beast and false prophet, the world religious leader portrayed in chapter 13, who along with the antichrist will unite all religions into one world religion. The seven hills where the woman rules indicates Rome which is noted for its seven hills, and also for seven world empires. These include (1) Assyria, (2) Egypt, (3) Medo-Persia, (4) Babylon, (5) Greece, (6) Rome and (7) the revived Roman empire. We are living in the day of this revived Roman empire, which is the current European Union.

Some believe that the one-world church will be the Catholic church, which has always been identified with Rome, and that the one-world church leader will the Pope, though not necessarily the present pope. There has long existed what many consider idolatry in the Catholic church in the practice of praying to Mary, and other "saints," instead of honoring Jesus Christ as the only mediator between God and man.

> *For there is one God and one Mediator*
> *between God and men, the Man Christ Jesus,*
> *who gave Himself a ransom for all, to be*
> *testified in due time...*

(1 Timothy 2:6, NKJV)

This is something to watch for as these things emerge on the world stage. However, I doubt that the Catholic church in itself is the totality of the apostate church, as almost every denomination or non-denomination has members that would fit the description of the Laodicean church (mentioned in this chapter, and described more fully in chapter five). And, of course, there are many dear, devoted Catholic brothers and sisters. Remember, we are not talking about people here; we are talking about a world system that will be both political and religious.

Satan is the ruling power behind both the antichrist and false prophet. The beast upon which the woman sits represents the antichrist and his world system, which will usher in the time of tribulation. The false prophet, or world

THE ANSWER BOOK *For Troubled Times*

religious leader, as mentioned before is instrumental in getting people to believe and worship the antichrist. When the antichrist arrives in his coveted place of being the world leader, he doesn't need this apostate church any longer, so he destroys her—and this world religious system.

Modern Babylon's materialism and immorality ends in destruction.

Chapter 18 shows a devastating turn of events. "Babylon," standing for the world system is filled with pride, covetousness, riches and materialism, wealthy trade, immorality and every kind of wickedness. God has given her repeated opportunities to repent and return to Him, but she does not. Look at what happens:

> *After all this I saw another angel come down from heaven with great authority, and the earth grew bright with his splendor. He gave a mighty shout: "Babylon is fallen—that great city is fallen!...For all the nations have fallen because of the wine of her passionate immorality. The kings of the world have committed adultery with her. Because of her desires for extravagant luxury, the merchants of the world have grown rich."*

(Revelation 18:1-3, NLT)

Who is "Babylon?" Bible prophecy experts disagree. Some think this refers to the European Union; others think it refers to Iraq, in which is located the site of the former city of Babylon; while still others have suggested that this is America. I do not personally believe America is the Babylon of Revelation, but as a country we certainly fit the description above and would do well to heed the Word of the Lord:

> *Then I heard another voice calling from*
> *heaven, "Come away from her, my people.*
> *Do not take part in her sins, or you will be*
> *punished with her. For her sins are piled as*
> *high as heaven...*
>
> (Revelation 18:4-5, NLT)

As Christians, we definitely need to be watchful that we do not fall into sin in these end times...that we stay true to our Lord Jesus Christ until the end, so that we may reign with Him forever. What punishment does Babylon receive?

> *Therefore, these plagues will overtake her in a*
> *single day— death and mourning and famine.*
> *She will be completely consumed by fire, for*
> *the Lord God who judges her is mighty." And*
> *the kings of the world who committed adultery*
> *with her and enjoyed her great luxury will*
> *mourn for her as they see the smoke rising*
> *from her charred remains. They will stand at a*
> *distance, terrified by her great torment.*
>
> (Revelation 18:8-10, NLT)

Again, I encourage you to read the entire chapter, indeed all of Revelation, as I have only been able to skim through portions of it in this book. Remember, at the beginning of this chapter, we learned that God gives a blessing to those who read, hear, and do what is contained in the book of Revelation.

The wedding supper of the Lamb

Chapter 19 begins with a vast crowd praising the Lord with songs of great victory!

> *6 Then I heard again what sounded like the shout of a vast crowd or the roar of mighty ocean waves or the crash of loud thunder: "Praise the Lord! For the Lord our God, the Almighty, reigns.*
>
> *7 Let us be glad and rejoice, and let us give honor to him. For the time has come for the wedding feast of the Lamb, and his bride has prepared herself.*
>
> *8 She has been given the finest of pure white linen to wear." For the fine linen represents the good deeds of God's holy people.*
>
> *9 And the angel said to me, "Write this: Blessed are those who are invited to the wedding feast of the Lamb." And he added, "These are true words that come from God."*
>
> (Revelation 19:6-9, NLT)

Believers, the body of Christ and the bride of Christ, are saved by grace through faith. From the beginning, it was ordained by God that those who believe in His Son Jesus would walk in good works. We are not judged for salvation on our works; only the grace of God saves us through our faith in the One He sent. But, there will be a reward in heaven that is based on the faithfulness and pure motives of our earthly works.

6 And God raised us up with Christ and seated us with him in the heavenly realms in Christ Jesus,

7 in order that in the coming ages he might show the incomparable riches of his grace, expressed in his kindness to us in Christ Jesus.

8 For it is by grace you have been saved, through faith—and this not from yourselves, it is the gift of God—

9 not by works, so that no one can boast.

10 For we are God's workmanship, created in Christ Jesus to do good works, which God prepared in advance for us to do.

(Ephesians 2:6-10, NIV)

The remainder of chapter 19 shows Jesus Christ riding regally on a white horse into battle with the antichrist, the false prophet, and the huge army of their followers.

Then I saw the beast and the kings of the world and their armies gathered together to fight against the one sitting on the horse and his army. And the beast was captured, and with him the false prophet who did mighty miracles on behalf of the beast—miracles that deceived all who had accepted the mark of the beast and who worshiped his statue. Both

*the beast and his false prophet were thrown
alive into the fiery lake of burning sulfur. Their
entire army was killed by the sharp sword that
came from the mouth of the one riding the
white horse...*

(Revelation 19:19-21, NLT)

Beware, my friend. Be sure that you are on the right side. Do not be deceived by the things that are to come. Receive Christ today, and stay close to Him both now and for eternity!

Satan is defeated and Judgment Day has come

Chapter 20 continues the story, showing that the dragon, satan, is chained in a bottomless pit for one thousand years. Then he is released only to cause more havoc on the earth until the time of his final demise.

*7 When the thousand years come to an end,
Satan will be let out of his prison.*

*8 He will go out to deceive the nations—called
Gog and Magog—in every corner of the earth.
He will gather them together for battle—a
mighty army, as numberless as sand along the
seashore.*

*9 And I saw them as they went up on the
broad plain of the earth and surrounded God's
people and the beloved city. But fire from
heaven came down on the attacking armies
and consumed them.*

10 Then the devil, who had deceived them,
was thrown into the fiery lake of burning
sulfur, joining the beast and the false prophet.
There they will be tormented day and night
forever and ever.

(Revelation 20:7-10, NLT)

Then, Judgment Day came for everyone—both great and small—upon the earth and under the earth. No one escaped the presence of Jesus, who was counted worthy to open the Book of Life and judge all by their deeds, good and bad.

The new heaven, the new earth,
and the new Jerusalem

Chapters 21 and 22 finish the book of Revelation but the world does not end, as many believe. Instead, there will be a new heaven and a new earth.

1 Then I saw a new heaven and a new earth,
for the old heaven and the old earth had
disappeared. And the sea was also gone.

2 And I saw the holy city, the new Jerusalem,
coming down from God out of heaven like a
bride beautifully dressed for her husband.

3 I heard a loud shout from the throne, saying,
"Look, God's home is now among his people!
He will live with them, and they will be his
people. God himself will be with them.

4 He will wipe every tear from their eyes,
and there will be no more death or sorrow

*or crying or pain. All these things are gone
forever."*

(Revelation 21:1-4, NLT)

Here is a partial description of the new Jerusalem, so
beautiful we cannot truly imagine its grandeur.

*18 The wall was made of jasper, and the city
was pure gold, as clear as glass.*

*19 The wall of the city was built on foundation
stones inlaid with twelve precious stones: the
first was jasper, the second sapphire, the third
agate, the fourth emerald,*

*20 the fifth onyx, the sixth carnelian, the
seventh chrysolite, the eighth beryl, the ninth
topaz, the tenth chrysoprase, the eleventh
jacinth, the twelfth amethyst.*

*21 The twelve gates were made of pearls—
each gate from a single pearl! And the main
street was pure gold, as clear as glass.*

*22 I saw no temple in the city, for the Lord
God Almighty and the Lamb are its temple.*

*23 And the city has no need of sun or moon,
for the glory of God illuminates the city, and
the Lamb is its light.*

(Revelation 21:18-23, NLT)

Jesus is coming soon! He is coming to take up His
Church to heaven where they will not experience the wrath
of God upon the earth during the tribulation hour. When
the wedding supper for believers of all ages is ready, He

will come again. Friend, if Jesus is your Savior and Lord, you will rule with Him in the new heaven and new earth and live in the magnificent city called the new Jerusalem. Be not so concerned with the matters of daily life and the riches of this world, which is passing away, but look up!

> *The Spirit and the bride say, "Come." Let anyone who hears this say, "Come." Let anyone who is thirsty come. Let anyone who desires drink freely from the water of life.*
>
> *He who is the faithful witness to all these things says, "Yes, I am coming soon!" Amen! Come, Lord Jesus!*

(Revelation 22:17, 20 NLT)

Chapter Three

America's Finest Hour:
A People of Courage and Faith Arise!

Now is not the time to point the finger of blame and accusation toward the Republicans, the Democrats, the enormous national debt, the war or wrong decisions and actions…but rather it is the time to stand as Americans to support each other and find answers that will work!

The Bible describes the condition of the human race in the last days of earth as we know it now.

> *But mark this: There will be terrible times in the last days. People will be lovers of themselves, lovers of money, boastful, proud, abusive, disobedient to their parents, ungrateful, unholy, without love, unforgiving, slanderous, without self-control, brutal, not lovers of the good, treacherous, rash, conceited, lovers of pleasure rather than lovers of God—*
>
> (2 Timothy 3:1-3, NIV)

We have already read in chapters one and two, about the terrible judgments that are soon to come upon the earth because of the sin of mankind. But, it is not too late. Turning from pride and poking an arrogant finger against God, and His people, can still yield positive results and save our country.

Let me tell you about a prideful king in the Old Testament that many of you have heard about. He lost his glory, kingdom and honor and was humbled by the God to whom he failed to give the credit for his greatness. This is a strong warning for any leader who feels he can run his country or kingdom without honoring the most high God and seeking His direction and plan for government.

A powerful king learns a lesson in humility

King Nebuchadnezzar had been given a strong and glorious kingdom by the God of heaven and earth. The king had great riches and supreme power over all of the people within his domain. He was very successful in conquering every land with which he made war.

King Nebuchadnezzar had a dream that troubled him greatly and called for all of the wise men, magicians and astrologers to tell him the dream because he had forgotten it as well as to interpret its meaning. Not one of these wise men could tell the dream, until one who was found who could: Daniel, a young Hebrew man, who worshiped the God of heaven and earth. Daniel credited God with giving him the meaning of the dream and said to the king, "I wish this dream was for your enemies and not for you."

But, the dream was meant for King Nebuchadnezzar, not his enemies, so Daniel proceeded to interpret the meaning at the command of the king. After he had first described the dream to the king, Daniel urged the king to turn to God, to become righteous and to do good to the poor, and maybe God would yet hold back His judgment that was evident in the dream. King Nebuchadnezzar continued in his prideful ways, ignoring Daniel's warning, and we see what happened next:

The Dream's Fulfillment

28 "But all these things did happen to King Nebuchadnezzar.

29 Twelve months later he was taking a walk on the flat roof of the royal palace in Babylon.

30 As he looked out across the city, he said, 'Look at this great city of Babylon! By my own mighty power, I have built this beautiful city as my royal residence to display my majestic splendor.'

31 "While these words were still in his mouth, a voice called down from heaven, 'O King Nebuchadnezzar, this message is for you! You are no longer ruler of this kingdom.

32 You will be driven from human society. You will live in the fields with the wild animals, and you will eat grass like a cow. Seven periods of time will pass while you live this way, until you learn that the Most High rules over the kingdoms of the world and gives them to anyone he chooses.'

*33 "That same hour the judgment was
fulfilled, and Nebuchadnezzar was driven from
human society. He ate grass like a cow, and he
was drenched with the dew of heaven. He lived
this way until his hair was as long as eagles'
feathers and his nails were like birds' claws.*

*34 "After this time had passed, I,
Nebuchadnezzar, looked up to heaven. My
sanity returned, and I praised and worshiped
the Most High and honored the one who lives
forever.*

*His rule is everlasting,
and his kingdom is eternal.*

*35 All the people of the earth are nothing
compared to him. He does as he pleases
among the angels of heaven and among the
people of the earth. No one can stop him or
say to him, What do you mean by doing these
things?'*

*36 "When my sanity returned to me, so did my
honor and glory and kingdom. My advisers
and nobles sought me out, and I was restored
as head of my kingdom, with even greater
honor than before.*

*37 "Now I, Nebuchadnezzar, praise and
glorify and honor the King of heaven. All his
acts are just and true, and he is able to humble
the proud."*

(Daniel 4:34-37, NLT)

Re-read verse 30 and you will see the root of the destruction that came to the king's life because of pride and the failure to give glory to God. Everything good we have in America, and in our own individual lives, comes from God. The book of John, in talking about Jesus, says there is nothing that has been created that was not created by Him (John 1:3). Your very breath is given to you by God. He can stop your heart in an instant and you will die. Then, where will all your glory be…all your magnificent acts?

Only a fool says, "There is no God!"

In the Psalms, there is a Scripture that says only a fool says there is no God (Psalm 53:1). Nebuchadnezzar finally came to his senses and made a wise choice. He recognized that God is sovereign above all things. This time it was the king who humbled himself; looking up to heaven, Nebuchadnezzar worshiped and praised God. Look at the result in verse 36. God returned to Nebuchadnezzar all of his honor, glory and kingdom. All that the king had lost was restored with even greater honor than before!

Presidents, kings, prime ministers, and all leaders upon the earth, take heed! Make the wise choice to honor and serve God, and let your decisions…your policies line up with the ways of God as shown in the Bible. If you do not do it on your own, with a right heart, you may prosper for a season, but a time will come where what you thought was so important, what is most valuable to you will be lost, including possibly your own soul.

God purposed that leaders would rule justly and sensibly. He promises His guidance and enabling power to the leader who will place his trust in God and give Him the glory for his success.

> *1 The king's heart is like a stream of water directed by the Lord; he guides it wherever he pleases.*
>
> *2 People may be right in their own eyes, but the Lord examines their heart.*
>
> *3 The Lord is more pleased when we do what is right and just than when we offer him sacrifices.*

(Proverbs 21:1-3, NIV)

America's overcoming victory will not be won through military strategies and weapons, but through her people recognizing that turning to God is their only hope.... through a spirit of humility, repentance, faith and prayer. 2 Chronicles 7:14-15 puts it this way:

> *... if my people, who are called by my name, will humble themselves and pray and seek my face and turn from their wicked ways, then will I hear from heaven and will forgive their sin and will heal their land. Now my eyes will be open and my ears attentive to the prayers offered in this place.*

(2 Chronicles 7:14-15, NIV)

When America's eyes are opened, she will run to God. We have a choice…it can be a willing act on our part, or it can come from a desperate heart, when all other hope is lost.

How should we pray?

The Bible gives clear and specific direction to pray for our leaders and for all people because this is the way to a life of peace and goodness. It doesn't matter whether your candidate won the election or not. It doesn't matter whether you agree with the way America is being governed. It is our God-given privilege and responsibility to join our hearts and voices together as a mighty prayer force that will change the direction of this nation and the world.

> *1 I urge you, first of all, to pray for all people. Ask God to help them; intercede on their behalf, and give thanks for them.*
>
> *2 Pray this way for kings and all who are in authority so that we can live peaceful and quiet lives marked by godliness and dignity.*
>
> *3 This is good and pleases God our Savior,*
>
> *4 who wants everyone to be saved and to understand the truth.*
>
> *5 For there is only one God and one Mediator who can reconcile God and humanity—the man Christ Jesus.*
>
> *6 He gave his life to purchase freedom for everyone. This is the message God gave to the world at just the right time.*

(1 Timothy 2:1-6, NLT)

A blessing or curse comes according to how you treat Israel

God judges nations based on how they treat Israel—whether they are for or against God's chosen people. Israel has been blessed by God. No enemy, no matter how formidable, can "curse" or successfully war against what God has blessed.

> *"I will bless those who bless* (Abraham and the nation of Israel), *and whoever curses you I will curse; and all peoples on earth will be blessed through you."*
>
> (Genesis 12:3, NIV)

Please understand that I am not saying that we, as Christian believers, should become enemies to the people dwelling in the nations who have historically and even presently exhibit hostility toward the Jewish people. We should not consider them any less valuable as people. They too are part of God's creation. God loves all people of every nation, race and creed the same. Jesus came first to give salvation to the Jews, but they rejected Him, so His salvation has been given to the gentiles, who by the millions are gratefully receiving His free gift of grace. The time will come though when the eyes of God's originally chosen people, the Jews, will be opened and they too will flock into the kingdom of God, receiving Jesus as their long-awaited Messiah. Hallelujah!

America needs to be sure her political agenda concerning Israel lines up with God's instructions in the

Bible; i.e., we should not coerce Israel to give up land that God has promised to them, any more than we should expect other nations to give up the land God has given to them.

The best ways that we, as a nation and as a church, can bless Israel is first of all, to show a demonstration of support toward them verbally and in our actions, pray for them, be kind to Jewish people (and all people) wherever they live—in Israel, America, or in other nations of the world, help them through missions work to provide food and other necessities for the poor and elderly, and in any other way that God shows us that we can support them.

God commands specifically in the Bible that we are to bless Israel and pray for their peace. As we do this, we can be sure the Lord is pleased and will prosper us in return.

> *Pray for peace in Jerusalem. May all who love this city prosper.*
>
> (Psalm 122:6, NLT)

He who lives by the sword, dies by the sword

Israel is not the only hotspot of tension in the world. Anger and disputes exist in many places in the world including our own beloved America. Fighting and protests will only fuel the fire of an already explosive situation. We do not want another Civil War in America, or pockets of revolution throughout our destitute, impoverished land. Love is greater than guns and missiles. True God-like, unconditional love will never fail.

Look at what Jesus told Peter, who thought that the answer to the immediate problem was violence—to cut off the ear of the offender:

> *But one of the men with Jesus pulled out*
> *his sword and struck the high priest's slave,*
> *slashing off his ear. "Put away your sword,"*
> *Jesus told him. "Those who use the sword will*
> *die by the sword.*
>
> (Matthew 26:51-52, NLT)

Are we a people of war…or are we a people of peace? Friend, in your own life and sphere of influence, do you "get your way" or "handle your problem" with a sword? Do you revert to anger or force? There is not space to include it here, but you will find a better way in Jesus' Sermon on the Mount in Matthew, chapter five. Jesus commends the "peacemakers" and those who are merciful, and applauds the humble, those not walking in pride and selfishness, whom He says will inherit the whole earth!

Christianity is often seen as a religion of intolerance and hate. This couldn't be further from the truth. In actuality, Christianity is founded on the selfless, sacrificial love of the God of the universe who sent His only begotten Son to die in your behalf and in my behalf for the punishment of our sins so that we could stand before a righteous God.

It's time to revolutionize your thinking

This book has been written in order to revolutionize your thinking about how to survive in troubled times. The natural tendency is to hoard…to hold on to everything you have so that you don't lose it. Some will go so far as to steal and commit crimes against their fellow Americans out of fear and desperation. But, it doesn't have to be that way.

> *For God has not given us a spirit of fear, but of power and of love and of a sound mind.*
> (2 Timothy 1:7, NKJV)

Friend, I'm here to tell you that God's "Give, and it shall be given unto you" approach to not only money, but every life commodity is not out-of-date. God's ways are not dead; they will lead not only to meager survival, but to spiritual, physical and material prosperity in the midst of famine and trouble.

A unique battle plan wins the victory!

There is a story in the Old Testament that illustrates the power of God, the ingenuity of God, and the limitless ways He has of accomplishing victory. The people of Israel were frightened and didn't know what to do because they were about to be attacked by an army many times larger than their own. So, the king and the people went before the Lord in earnest, heart-felt prayer and fasting. God heard their prayers. Let's pick up the Scripture from here:

> *14 Then the Spirit of the LORD came upon Jahaziel the son of Zechariah, the son of Benaiah, the son of Jeiel, the son of Mattaniah, a Levite of the sons of Asaph, in the midst of the assembly.*

15 And he said, "Listen, all you of Judah and you inhabitants of Jerusalem, and you, King Jehoshaphat! Thus says the LORD to you: 'Do not be afraid nor dismayed because of this great multitude, for the battle is not yours, but God's.

16 Tomorrow go down against them. They will surely come up by the Ascent of Ziz, and you will find them at the end of the brook before the Wilderness of Jeruel.

17 You will not need to fight in this battle. Position yourselves, stand still and see the salvation of the LORD, who is with you, O Judah and Jerusalem!' Do not fear or be dismayed; tomorrow go out against them, for the LORD is with you."

18 And Jehoshaphat bowed his head with his face to the ground, and all Judah and the inhabitants of Jerusalem bowed before the LORD, worshiping the LORD.

19 Then the Levites of the children of the Kohathites and of the children of the Korahites stood up to praise the LORD God of Israel with voices loud and high.

20 So they rose early in the morning and went out into the Wilderness of Tekoa; and as they went out, Jehoshaphat stood and said, "Hear me, O Judah and you inhabitants of Jerusalem: Believe in the LORD your God, and you shall be established; believe His prophets, and you shall prosper."

21 And when he had consulted with the people, he appointed those who should sing to the LORD, and who should praise the beauty of holiness, as they went out before the army and were saying:

"Praise the LORD,
For His mercy endures forever."

22 Now when they began to sing and to praise, the LORD set ambushes against the people of Ammon, Moab, and Mount Seir, who had come against Judah; and they were defeated.

23 For the people of Ammon and Moab stood up against the inhabitants of Mount Seir to utterly kill and destroy them. And when they had made an end of the inhabitants of Seir, they helped to destroy one another.

24 So when Judah came to a place overlooking the wilderness, they looked toward the multitude; and there were their dead bodies, fallen on the earth. No one had escaped.

25 When Jehoshaphat and his people came to take away their spoil, they found among them an abundance of valuables on the dead bodies, and precious jewelry, which they stripped off for themselves, more than they could carry away; and they were three days gathering the spoil because there was so much.

26 And on the fourth day they assembled in the Valley of Berachah, for there they blessed the LORD; therefore the name of that place was called The Valley of Berachah until this day.

27 Then they returned, every man of Judah and Jerusalem, with Jehoshaphat in front of them, to go back to Jerusalem with joy, for the LORD had made them rejoice over their enemies.

28 So they came to Jerusalem, with stringed instruments and harps and trumpets, to the house of the LORD.

29 And the fear of God was on all the kingdoms of those countries when they heard that the LORD had fought against the enemies of Israel.

30 Then the realm of Jehoshaphat was quiet, for his God gave him rest all around.

(2 Chronicles 20:14-30, NKJV)

Now, I am not suggesting that we send out a group of praise singers in place of the United States military forces; however, I do believe this favorite story in the Old Testament is an excellent example of when a people seeks God, places their trust and hope in Him, and is willing to follow His marching orders, they can win no matter how fearsome or big the enemy may seem.

Today, in the midst of terror and threats of harm, people are fearful to walk down the streets, nervously peering behind them looking for danger. America's streets may not always be safe, but you can rest in the knowledge that you personally can be safe…your family can be safe, if you are truly trusting in the Lord.

The Scriptures are full of promises of protection and safety when we place our trust in the Lord. Jesus admonished his disciples and the people many times to "fear not." Following are two of my favorite verses. If you commit them to memory, then whenever fear threatens to engulf you, you can speak them out confidently. You will find this confession will bring peace to your mind and heart.

> *The fear of man brings a snare. But whoever trusts in the LORD shall be safe.*
>
> (Proverbs 29:25, NKJV)

> *For God has not given us a spirit of fear, but of power and of love and of a sound mind.*
>
> (2 Timothy 1:7, NKJV)

America, it is time for the glory of God to be poured out on you!

The glory is God's presence, His power, and all that He is. The Bible promises that God's glory will cover the earth.

> *For the earth will be filled With the knowledge of the glory of the LORD, As the waters cover the sea.*
>
> (Habakkuk 2:14, NKJV)

Just like Lazarus, God is Able to Raise America from the Dead!

Jesus also carries the glory of God. Look at this story in the Bible about His friends Lazarus, Mary and Martha, a great example of the glory of God in action. Lazarus, the brother of Mary and Martha, became sick and died. Word was sent to Jesus because He loved this family, and everybody had expected Jesus to heal Lazarus. But Jesus waited a few days until after Lazarus had already died. Let's pick the Scripture up here:

38 Jesus, once more deeply moved, came to the tomb. It was a cave with a stone laid across the entrance.

39 "Take away the stone," he said. "But, Lord," said Martha, the sister of the dead man, "by this time there is a bad odor, for he has been there four days."

40 Then Jesus said, "Did I not tell you that if you believed, you would see the glory of God?"

41 So they took away the stone. Then Jesus looked up and said, "Father, I thank you that you have heard me.

42 I knew that you always hear me, but I said this for the benefit of the people standing here, that they may believe that you sent me."

43 When he had said this, Jesus called in a loud voice, "Lazarus, come out!"

44 The dead man came out, his hands and feet wrapped with strips of linen, and a cloth around his face.

Jesus said to them, "Take off the grave clothes and let him go."

(John 11:38-44, NIV)

100

America's answer lies in God who created all of heaven and earth. The Creator, like any manufacturer, has given us an owner's manual, which is called *The Holy Bible.* This is God's written word.

> *This* (Bible—both Old and New Testaments) *shall not depart from your mouth, but you shall meditate in it day and night, that you may observe to do according to all that is written in it. For then you will make your way prosperous, and then you will have good success.*
>
> (Joshua 1:8, NKJV)

This same Creator not only sent us His Word (of life, instruction, success) in written form, but He sent His Word in "living" form, which is Jesus Christ.

> *And the Word* (Jesus Christ) *became flesh and dwelt among us, and we beheld His glory, the glory as of the only begotten of the Father, full of grace and truth.*
>
> (John 1:14, NKJV)

God sent His Word—both His written and living Word—to mankind for our benefit. God's Word brings salvation, healing, freedom, and all God wants is for man to recognize His kindness and deep desire to bless man with goodness and mercy.

> *He sent His word and healed them, And delivered them from their destructions. Oh,*

*that men would give thanks to the LORD for
His goodness, And for His wonderful works to
the children of men!*

(Psalm 107:20-21, NKJV)

God, as a good Father, corrects those He loves

*I correct and discipline everyone I love. So
be diligent and turn from your indifference.
"Look! I stand at the door and knock. If you
hear my voice and open the door, I will come
in, and we will share a meal together as
friends. Those who are victorious will sit with
me on my throne, just as I was victorious and
sat with my Father on his throne.*

(Revelation 3:19-21, NLT)

If God speaks such a grand invitation to those who already believe, how much more fervently will He speak to those for whom He also longs to come to Himself, who have yet to make the decision to open the door of their hearts and lives to Christ?

It is not too late…even in the midst of famine, God will bless those who honor Him as their Lord and obey His directions. Look what happened to Isaac in the Old Testament in just such a situation:

*1 Now there was a famine in the land—besides
the earlier famine of Abraham's time—and
Isaac went to Abimelech king of the Philistines
in Gerar.*

2 The LORD appeared to Isaac and said, "Do not go down to Egypt; live in the land where I tell you to live.

3 Stay in this land for a while, and I will be with you and will bless you…

12 Isaac planted crops in that land and the same year reaped a hundredfold, because the LORD blessed him.

(Genesis 26:1-3, 12, NIV)

Our foundation for spiritual and physical survival can be built on nothing less that the Savior God sent. God never changes, never adds a "new way," and the message is still the same. Paul plainly proclaimed to the Corinthians this truth:

1 When I came to you, brothers, I did not come with eloquence or superior wisdom as I proclaimed to you the testimony about God.

2 For I resolved to know nothing while I was with you except Jesus Christ and him crucified.

3 I came to you in weakness and fear, and with much trembling.

4 My message and my preaching were not with wise and persuasive words, but with a demonstration of the Spirit's power,

5 so that your faith might not rest on men's wisdom, but on God's power.

(1 Corinthians 2:1-5, NIV)

And Paul continues with this message in the next chapter:

> *By the grace God has given me, I laid a*
> *foundation as an expert builder, and someone*
> *else is building on it. But each one should be*
> *careful how he builds. For no one can lay any*
> *foundation other than the one already laid,*
> *which is Jesus Christ.*
>
> (1 Corinthians 3:10-11, NIV)

This is true for every individual human being, no matter where they live or what they have been brought up to believe in the past. Not only is this the criteria for "survival," but it will bring spiritual, physical and material prosperity into your life—and into your country. If America is to survive and prosper in her "finest hour," she too will have to build upon the foundation of Jesus Christ!

Your future depends on the choice you make

You have read much about the importance of turning to God—both as a nation and as individuals. Our future as a nation, whether destruction or blessing, will depend on the choices of the Ameican people. Those who have chosen to follow Christ, even though they may be in the minority, have a power greater than any world leader, Hollywood star, champion athlete, great businessman or others who may be successful in the world's eyes. When it comes to a Christian who is faithful to pray for their country and its leaders, there is no numbers game. One Christian, plus God, is a majority! How much more can we accomplish in turning America and her people in the right direction—back to God—when we join together as the people of God to pray, and by our examples, to "love the lost into the kingdom of heaven."

As individuals, each person has a choice to make, a life or death decision, which will determine their eternal destiny. My friend, read carefully the following words; these are not for the Jew only, but for all people everywhere. This Scripture says that the choice to love and obey the Lord, is the key to your life!

> *"Today I have given you the choice between life and death, between blessings and curses. Now I call on heaven and earth to witness the choice you make. Oh, that you would choose life, so that you and your descendants might live! You can make this choice by loving the LORD your God, obeying him, and committing yourself firmly to him. This is the key to your life. And if you love and obey the LORD, you will live long in the land the LORD swore to give your ancestors Abraham, Isaac, and Jacob."*
>
> (Deuteronomy 30:19-20, NLT)

Trusting in God alone brings victory!

Yes, the answer for America is to return to God. . . the God of her founding fathers… through Jesus Christ. But, turning to God is a choice, a decision that the government cannot make for us. It is a decision that each individual person must make for themselves.

Turning to God is a matter of the heart, not of the mind. Because it involves a trust that means you surrender your own self-will and your own self-effort to a God who knows all. He knows all, not only about things like the universe; He knows all about you. After all, He created you. He knows the path and has the plan that will bring the greatest meaning and joy to your life, if only you will place your trust in Him. Take His hand; let Him guide you, and you will find greater fulfillment, success and peace in every area of your life than you could ever dream up on your own, much less accomplish through your own human strategies and abilities.

One of the major problems people have in turning to God, especially Americans with our self-sufficient pride, is the fear that God will lead us into something terrible and unpleasant. Nothing could be further from the truth. Even Christians sometimes have trouble fully letting go of the reigns and handing their future over to their heavenly Father.

But, I assure you my friend, God's plans are good. When you step into His destiny for you, you will wonder why you ever doubted, why you ever waited to say, "Yes" to God.

> *For I know the plans I have for you," declares*
> *the LORD, "plans to prosper you and not to*
> *harm you, plans to give you hope and a future.*
> *Then you will call upon me and come and*
> *pray to me, and I will listen to you.*

(Jeremiah 29:11-12, NIV)

106

When I was eight or nine years old, often instead of being outside playing with the other children in the neighborhood, I would be sitting inside the house thinking up stories. I loved to write and wanted to be a writer when I grew up. Time passed, hard times came, and I took a different direction from my childhood dreams. But, one day after I received Christ into my life, God opened an unexpected, miraculous door which gave me the opportunity to get started in the writing field despite my not having any real qualifications. I am still there today, working my "dream." So, you see, the plans of God are good! Just ask Him in prayer today if there isn't some secret dream in your heart that He will ignite with His power and grace, and bring into glorious reality. You may be surprised that God's plans for you are much more exciting and more fulfilling than your plans for you!

If things aren't going your way today and you are facing serious challenges, pour out your heart to the Father, just as you would to your earthly parents. If you didn't have a caring and supportive earthly father, or you didn't know your earthly father, you can know for sure that God will not disappoint you like earthly parents sometimes do. God is Love and love never fails!

A Ladder to the Clouds

(Excerpted from The Prayer of Jabez © by Exponential, Inc. Used by permission of WaterBrook Multnomah Publishing Group, a division of Random House, Inc.)

Dr. Bruce Wilkinson, author of the best-selling book *The Prayer of Jabez*, which has sold over nine-million copies since its release, shares a personal experience in his book on the lesson of trust:

"One day when our kids were preschoolers, Darlene and I found ourselves with them at a large city park in southern California. It was the kind of park that makes a grown man wish he were a kid again. It had swings, monkey bars, and seesaws, but what was most enticing were the slides—not just one slide, but three—from small, to medium, to enormous. David, who was five at the time, took off like a shot for the small slide.

"Why don't you go down with him?" Darlene suggested.

But I had another idea. "Let's wait and see what happens," I said. So we relaxed on a nearby bench and watched. David clambered happily to the top of the smallest slide. He waved over at us with a big smile, then whizzed down.

Without hesitation he moved over to the medium-sized slide. He had climbed halfway up the ladder when he turned and looked at me. I looked away. He pondered his options for a moment, then carefully backed down one step at a time.

"Honey, you ought to go help him out," my wife said.

"Not yet," I replied, hoping the twinkle in my eye would reassure her that I wasn't just being careless.

David spent a few minutes at the bottom of the middle slide watching other kids climb up, whiz down, and run around to do it again. Finally his little mind was made up.

He could do it. He climbed up…and slid down. Three times, in fact, without even looking at us.

Then we watched him turn and head toward the highest slide. Now Darlene was getting anxious. "Bruce, I don't think he should do that by himself, do you?"

"No," I replied as calmly as possible. "But I don't think he will. Let's see what he does."

When David reached the bottom of the giant slide, he turned and called out, "Daddy!" But I glanced away again, pretending I couldn't hear him.

He peered up the ladder. In his young imagination, it must have reached to the clouds. He watched a teenage boy go hurtling down the slide. Then, against all odds, he decided to try. Step-by-step, hand over hand, he inched up the ladder. He hadn't reached a third of the way when he froze. By this time, the teenager was coming up behind him and yelled at him to get going. But David couldn't. He couldn't go up or down. He had reached the point of certain failure.

I rushed over. "Are you okay, son?" I asked from the bottom of the ladder.

He looked down at me, shaken but clinging to that ladder with steely determination. And I could tell he had a question ready.

"Dad, will you come down the slide with me?" he asked. The teenager was losing patience, but I wasn't about to let the moment go.

"Why son?" I asked, peering up into his little face.

"I can't do it without you, Dad," he said, trembling. "It's too big for me!"

I stretched as high as I could to reach him and lifted him into my arms. Then we climbed that long ladder up to the clouds together. At the top, I put my son between my legs and wrapped my arms around him. Then we went zipping down the slide together, laughing all the way."

(Dr. Wilkinson continues in his world-famous book *The Prayer of Jabez* about the lesson of trust illustrated in this fun, but growth-inspiring adventure he and his wife had with their little son.):

His Hand, His Spirit

That is what your Father's hand is like. You tell Him, "Father, please do this in me because I can't do it alone! It's too big for me!" And you step out in faith to say and do things that could only come from His hand. Afterwards, your spirit is shouting, God did that, nobody else! God carried me, gave me the words, gave me the power—and it is wonderful!

I couldn't recommend more highly living in this supernatural dimension!

God's power under us, in us, surging through us is exactly what turns dependence into unforgettable experiences of completeness. "Not that we are sufficient of ourselves," wrote Paul, "to think of anything as being from ourselves, but our sufficiency is from God, who also made us sufficient as ministers of the new covenant." (2 Corinthians 3:5-6).

It's time to be real!

Friend, are you tired of fitting into the mold manufactured by society? Tired of being pressured to "have it all under control all of the time?" Tired of pretending that "I'm ok" when things are not ok…when inside you are feeling insecure, afraid of failure, and wondering what to do next?

In these fearful, uncertain times of economic crisis and lack, it's ok to be real. It's ok to say, "God, I need Your help." With God, you can take off the mask. Jesus admonished His disciples of the importance of coming to God like little children. He didn't mean being childish, but in a simplicity of faith and trust that with "Dad" things are going to be all right. God's Word promises that He will never leave you or forsake you.

You don't have to stay in a fearful state. When Jesus Christ lives in you in a born-again experience, you can be strong and have a confidence that comes from God. Jesus said that we are more than conquerors in Him (Romans 8:37), and that we can overcome (all the trials of) the world by our faith in Jesus Christ (1 John 5:4).

Safety comes from trusting in the Lord. You don't have to suffer with anxiety or insomnia.

> *I will lie down and sleep in peace, for you alone, O LORD, make me dwell in safety.*
>
> (Psalm 4:8, NIV)

Peace comes from trusting in the Lord. God will share with you His divine direction and wisdom when you place your trust in Him:

> *Trust in the Lord with all your heart; do not depend on your own understanding. Seek his will in all you do, and he will show you which path to take.*
>
> (Proverbs 29:25, NLT)

Strength comes from trusting in the Lord. God will shield you from trouble and help you in times of danger and fear.

> *The LORD is my strength and my shield; my heart trusts in him, and I am helped...*
>
> (Psalm 28:7, NIV)

Like a little child, pray with me now, "Father, I refuse to wallow in self-pity and cower in fear no matter what is going on around me. I place my trust in You, knowing that you will never let me down. In Jesus' Name, Amen."

If you do not know Jesus as your personal Savior and Lord, see chapter nine *Departing for Heaven at "Gate*

Jesus": Don't Miss Your Departure Time! Then, you can joyfully enter into an exciting and secure Dad-son or Dad-daughter relationship with God that will bring safety, peace and strength to your life.

Chapter Four

The Church's Finest Hour: Joseph's Storehouse and Other Remedies

It's been said by many pastors and teachers that we are living in the Church's finest hour…

Dark will become darker, more evil and sinister than ever before. Murders, terrible abuse of every kind including sexual abuse such as rape, molesting defenseless little children, beatings, and conspiracies of men will abound everywhere. Crimes, such as assault and theft, will be on the rise as America's, and the world's, economic situation drives ordinary citizens to resort to stealing and violence to feed their families.

I am amazed at the growing rage of motorists over the simplest annoyances. Frustrated and impatient, they honk their horns for minutes on end and are ready to start a fight with their fellow drivers at the least provocation. In my car one day, I was sitting at a stoplight and observed the driver next to me, who was adamantly honking his horn non-stop, his face beet-red, cursing with obnoxious hand motions. Filled with compassion toward the man, I prayed for him, concerned that at any moment he might drop dead from a heart attack.

Though just a minor incident, this type of violent reaction results from feeling helpless in uncontrollable circumstances, and is indeed indicative of the increasing trend of human hopelessness—even among Christians— that ultimately leads to violence, and even death.

But, God's Word promises that as the world gets more sinful, grace will increase still greater than ever before. My brothers and sisters in Christ, we are entering into the time of the greatest revival in history. People need answers, and we have the Answer!

> *God's law was given so that all people could*
> *see how sinful they were. But as people*
> *sinned more and more, God's wonderful*
> *grace became more abundant. So just as*
> *sin ruled over all people and brought them*
> *to death, now God's wonderful grace rules*
> *instead, giving us right standing with God and*
> *resulting in eternal life through Jesus Christ*
> *our Lord.*
>
> (Romans 5:19-21, NLT)

As you know, we are living in times like none before— spiritually, politically and economically—with the threat of nuclear strike at our coasts and internally, economic upheaval is mounting daily. With our faith in God, in spite of the imminent dangers, we believe that America will stand! I believe this is the hour where the Church must take her place as a "trumpet blower" and as the instrument of God's saving grace and power.

The Church must play a strategic part in sounding the alarm, and organizing a harmony of efforts between churches to fulfill Christ's mandate of love by meeting end-time needs. This will open up a widespread opportunity for people to turn to the Lord and become born-again.

Church, God has set before you an open door that no man can shut through the tragic circumstances occurring in America.

> *"I know your works. See, I have set before you an open door, and no one can shut it; for you have a little strength, have kept My word, and have not denied My name.*

(Revelation 3:8, NKJV)

A call to love

God is Love. Love is the foundation upon which our outreach must be based if we are to be representatives of our Lord to a lost and hurting world. Following is a brief collection of "love" Scriptures and thoughts to meditate upon that will help build a sense of urgency and compassion in your heart to make a difference in America, and in the world.

> *If I could speak all the languages of earth and of angels, but didn't love others, I would only be a noisy gong or a clanging cymbal. If*

117

*I had the gift of prophecy, and if I understood
all of God's secret plans and possessed all
knowledge, and if I had such faith that I could
move mountains, but didn't love others, I
would be nothing If I gave everything I have to
the poor (out of duty only, without truly loving
them) and even sacrificed my body, I could
boast about it; but if I didn't love others, I
would have gained nothing.*

(1 Corinthians 13:1-3, NLT)

God commands each one of us in the Church to
love our neighbor as much as we love ourselves. This
commandment is second only to loving God Himself!
How important it is to Him that we consider the needs of
our neighbor—family, friend, coworker, and anyone we
meet, whether we know them personally or not—as being
as important as we consider our own. If you were hungry,
needed gas for your vehicle, or had some other vital need,
would you want someone to help? Of course, we all would!

*And you shall love the LORD your God with
all your heart, with all your soul, with all
your mind, and with all your strength.' This
is the first commandment. And the second,
like it, is this: 'You shall love your neighbor
as yourself.' There is no other commandment
greater than these."*

(Mark 12:30-31, NKJV)

*I am the Vine; you are the branches.
Whoever lives in Me and I in him bears much*

*(abundant) fruit. However, apart from Me
[cut off from vital union with Me] you can do
nothing. No one has greater love [no one has
shown stronger affection] than to lay down
(give up) his own life for his friends.*

(John 15: 5, 13, AMP)

o   The greatest love is loving others, preferring them,
    considering their needs even before our own.
o   We must abide in Jesus because we can do nothing
    apart from Jesus' enabling power in us.
o   As we abide in Jesus' love, we will grow in God's
    grace and wisdom.

Where is your treasure?

*Store your treasures in heaven, where moths
and rust cannot destroy, and thieves do not
break in and steal. Wherever your treasure is,
there the desires of your heart will also be.*

(Matthew 6: 20-21, NLT)

o   On earth, material possessions are temporary; they
    only last for a little while, and are subject to breaking,
    wearing out, getting used up, or being destroyed.
o   In heaven, your treasure is eternal. When our focus is
    on helping others and caring about the eternal destiny
    of their souls, our treasure can never be stolen, lost,
    misused or destroyed. This treasure we will be able to
    enjoy forever!

Jesus Himself is our model for giving, for being kind, for lending a helping hand toward others. Again and again in the New Testament, before Jesus fed the multitudes, rescued his disciples from danger, healed the sick and set the captives free, countless times the Scripture says, "Jesus was moved with compassion, and…"

Church, Christian believer…are you moved with compassion today—the compassion of Jesus—to sacrifice some of your worldly goods, to share a kind word or prayer, to give of your time and money to a cause that is bigger than yourself and your needs?

Calling all churches….

How can the Church help? The Church is made up of all Christian believers worldwide. Each of us individually is responsible for our part in the "Great Commission" Jesus has given to us. This is our opportunity to win multitudes of precious souls to our Lord and to the kingdom of God.

There are many ways we as the corporate Body of Christ, the local church, and as individual Christians can help turn America back to God, meet the needs of those who are suffering, and lead millions of souls into eternal life with Jesus Christ during these dark, difficult days. Never before, have we had such an incredible opportunity to turn people from darkness to light, and from satan's kingdom to God's kingdom than we do now.

No matter what the circumstances seem to be in the world situation, we as Christians have a hope in Jesus

Christ that is beyond anything the world can say or do to us. Remember to look up, for your redemption draws near. But, as we stay focused on the coming of the Lord, our eternal hope, we don't want to lose sight of all the hurting, lost, confused, fearful people that Christ died for and also wants to bring into His kingdom.

We must set aside our own fear, temptation to isolate ourselves or hold on to what we have. Now is the time to show the love of God by sharing what we have, speaking words of hope and life, and doing what we can do to help others.

Do not panic or lose faith in God! You don't have to worry about *"how* God will provide" or even *"if* He will provide." God knows what your needs are. He hasn't forgotten or forsaken you. Be at peace in Him. When we have kingdom priorities and our hearts are right before God, His promise is clear:

> *But seek (aim at and strive after) first of all*
> *His kingdom and His righteousness (His*
> *way of doing and being right), and then all*
> *these things taken together will be given you*
> *besides.*

(Matthew 6:33, AMP)

The Bible says that it is impossible to please God without faith! Faith is our number one ally in today's world. Without it, we will not only fail to please God, we will not be able to receive from Him the supernatural provision of our needs.

121

And without faith it is impossible to please
God, because anyone who comes to him must
believe that he exists and that he rewards
those who earnestly seek him.

(Hebrews 11:6, NIV)

Love should be our primary motive and motivator…to care…to act in compassion…and to give…as God directs our heart and priorities. Be sensitive to the small, still voice of God inside of you that will alert you to opportunities to help someone by sharing the love of God with them in both spiritual and practical ways.

A wonderful promise from God's Word

When you help others who are in need, God promises that you yourself will not be in want. This is a greater insurance policy against loss and lack than any insurance policy that man has to offer.

He who gives to the poor will lack nothing,
but he who closes his eyes to them receives
many curses.

(Proverbs 28: 27, NIV)

God also promises that He will bless us through our unselfish giving to His Church, other Christian ministries and charitable organizations. "Give, and you shall receive" is a principle taught widely in the Church, but it also works in other spheres of life as well. Have you ever noticed that most rich people are also generous, giving people?

Jewish people are known the world over for being astute business men, inventors, and great politicians. You will find them having great success everywhere—in the medical profession, the creative arts, media, entertainment, education, science and just about every other field of endeavor. Did you ever wonder why? The Jews are the chosen people of God and God has blessed them!

And, when we get into agreement with God and bless the Jews and Israel, we also will be blessed by God.

In addition, the Jews have been taught the system of tithing from their earliest years. This is giving a tenth of all their increase as directed by their religious law. Look at the magnificent results that come from tithing and giving offerings:

> *Bring all the tithes (the whole tenth of your income) into the storehouse, that there may be food in My house, and prove Me now by it, says the Lord of hosts, if I will not open the windows of heaven for you and pour you out a blessing, that there shall not be room enough to receive it. And I will rebuke the devourer [insects and plagues] for your sakes and he shall not destroy the fruits of your ground, neither shall your vine drop its fruit before the time in the field, says the Lord.*
>
> (Malachi 3: 10-11, AMP)

A matter of grace, not law

Today, in the Christian Church, many believers also tithe because they want to support God's work and also receive the same blessings as Abraham! Tithing in the Christian Church is not a matter of law, but of grace in honor of our Lord Jesus Christ. We are to give as God lays on our hearts to a church, to charities, to the widows and orphans. This may be in increments of 1%, 10% 30% or more of our income and resources—whatever God tells you personally to give. If you love the Lord and want to bless people, you will want to give. You'll be looking for opportunities and ways to give more, not to give less. Be led by the Holy Spirit…the still, small voice of God in your heart.

> *Suppose you see a brother or sister who has no food or clothing, and you say, "Good-bye and have a good day; stay warm and eat well"—but then you don't give that person any food or clothing. What good does that do? So you see, faith by itself isn't enough. Unless it produces good deeds, it is dead and useless.*

> (James 2:15-17, NLT)

The principle of tithing works not only with money, but with food, volunteering our time, prayer, a room for the homeless, buying a tank of gas for someone else, making their car payment this month if they are out of a job… every good thing we have to give. The Lord is pleased when we share a portion of our resources with those in need. The greatest gift we can give is to share Jesus with someone who doesn't know Him. The blessing of God will come back to us eternally and when we and our families are in need. In addition, we will have the warm, beautiful feeling of satisfaction that we have done something that has benefited others who are hurting.

A little note here…it is God who gives us everything we have, so we want to be very careful to give Him the glory for any good thing we do. It is not in ourselves that we are able to do these things, but through the goodness and provision of God. Jesus is honored when our motives are pure.

If we all do our part as believers, and those who love Christ, we can have more than enough for everyone. In the New Covenant, giving is a privilege, not a commandment, but I think if we follow the 10% example from the Old Testament (mentioned previously in this chapter), or even more as God provides and moves on our hearts, there will be ample provision to get through the troubled times we are living in. And…**This will be a great opportunity to show people that God is good, and lead many of them to our loving Provider!**

However, as important as faith is, God gives us wisdom, both spiritually and naturally. This chapter is meant to encourage churches to step up, organize and operate centers of hope, which will provide food and help not only for congregation members but also for community members. (See chapter seven *Especially for Pastors: A Message and*

Model for information on how churches can be centers of prayer, healing and equipping believers in ministry and spiritual gifts. You will also find an in-depth description of a church food ministry operation in that chapter.)

God can promote you
from the prison to the palace

You will find in the first book of the Bible, Genesis, a fascinating story about Joseph, the dreamer, the favored son of his father, Jacob. Joseph's father gave him a very special gift, a coat of many colors, which was the envy of his ten brothers. If you don't know the story, you need to read it! But, to make it short here for the sake of space, let if suffice to say that Joseph's jealous brothers sold him into slavery, and he was taken bound to the land of Egypt. Though Joseph was faithful in the duties assigned to him, he later wound up in prison for a crime he didn't commit.

The pharaoh's baker and butler had also been thrown into the same prison and they became troubled over dreams they had. Joseph was able to give the interpretation of both dreams accurately. The pharaoh himself had two dreams that he couldn't understand. He eagerly sought someone who could interpret the dreams. The chief butler, who had been released from prison and restored to his position, remembered Joseph's ability to understand dreams and told the pharaoh about him.

Joseph was summoned from prison and God gave him the interpretation of Pharaoh's dreams. The meaning of the dreams indicated that there would be seven years of plenty, then seven years of famine in the land of Egypt (which, in the Bible, signifies the "world").

"What shall we do?" asked Pharaoh.

Joseph suggested that he appoint a man to oversee a plan to establish a storehouse of food during the years of plenty, so that there would be enough during the years of famine. Pharaoh appointed Joseph, who became second in command next to Pharaoh himself, over all the land of Egypt. When the years of famine arrived, people came from the neighboring nations to get grain from Egypt because this was the only place in which there was a surplus of food. Among those who came were Joseph's brothers, who were eventually reunited with Joseph. Joseph moved his family to this land of plenty, and Pharaoh gave Joseph's father, brothers and all of their families the best land in Egypt .

Even though his older brothers had betrayed him, Joseph extended forgiveness and grace to the brothers when they brought his younger brother, Benjamin, back with them to the land of Egypt. We are living in an extended time of grace, where God's love and mercy are reaching out to the lost and hurting in these perilous times through the fearful days looming ahead for the entire earth.

Joseph's life, betrayal, and position of "savior" of the Hebrew people is a major type of Jesus.

Are we the last generation before Jesus returns?

It has been said that we are living in the generation of Benjamin, Joseph's younger brother. "Most Christians know the end-time generation to be the Joshua Generation. However, few are aware that we are also the Benjamin Generation," says Joseph Prince, noted minister and psalmist. "For just like Benjamin was the youngest and final son of Jacob, this generation will be God's last and final one before the rapture."

Joseph and Benjamin are powerful "types" for the plan of God in these end times. Jesus described the things that are close at hand, happening even now in many places:

> *You will hear of wars and rumors of wars, but*
> *see to it that you are not alarmed. Such things*
> *must happen, but the end is still to come.*
> *Nation will rise against nation, and kingdom*
> *against kingdom. There will be famines and*
> *earthquakes in various places. All these are*
> *the beginning of birth pains.*

(Matthew 24:6-8, NIV)

The economy is crashing all around us and famines will no longer be limited to third-world countries. Soon, we are coming into a time of worldwide famine, which will even affect our beloved United States of America. In addition, the fuel crisis increases. I also believe we will come into a place where even healthcare, in spite of—or maybe because of—plans for national healthcare, will fail. People will have to turn to their local church. They will have to trust God for the most basic of what most people now consider necessities.

As Joseph came up with a God-inspired plan to "save" his people and the people of Egypt (remember, a type of the world), the local church can become instrumental in meeting the needs of people—and leading them to salvation in Jesus Christ.

The "Joseph" vision for today

54 ...Then the seven years of famine began, just as Joseph had predicted. The famine also struck all the surrounding countries, but throughout Egypt there was plenty of food.

55 Eventually, however, the famine spread throughout the land of Egypt as well. And when the people cried out to Pharaoh for food, he told them, "Go to Joseph, and do whatever he tells you."

56 So with severe famine everywhere, Joseph opened up the storehouses and distributed grain to the Egyptians, for the famine was severe throughout the land of Egypt.

57 And people from all around came to Egypt to buy grain from Joseph because the famine was severe throughout the world.

(Genesis 41:54-57, NLT)

In the Scripture portion above, I am likening—in the current day situation—Egypt to the world, and Joseph to the Church in several ways:

(1) Just like God revealed to Joseph the meaning of Pharaoh's dreams and foretold of the devastation that lay ahead for the Egyptians (the world), the Church needs to sound the alarm…with the same message that was proclaimed by John the Baptist, and then Jesus: "Repent for the kingdom of heaven is at hand."

(2) When the famine struck the land, the Egyptians (the world) would have had no answers, except that they were prepared with God's plan in place. It was no longer business as usual. None of their natural systems or resources were adequate. In the coming economic climate, neither the government, nor the banks, oil companies or other corporations will have the ability to solve the crisis. This, in part, will set the stage for the appearance of the antichrist, who through the one-world government and one-world church will bring peace to Israel and the world—for a season.

But I believe that before the time of the antichrist's rule and blasphemy, the church will have an unprecedented opportunity for evangelism and revival—with the greatest outpouring of the Holy Spirit as well as sharing the "practical" demonstration of God's love. Jesus told His followers that the world would know they were His because of their love for one another.

(3) To whom did the leader of the land (Pharaoh) send the people for help? He sent them to Joseph

(the Church)! Joseph was prepared with the plan of God, and we as the Church need to be ready too for this great influx of people God will entrust to our care.

What did Joseph (as my example of the Church in this illustration) do to save his family, the children of Israel, and the people of Egypt and its neighboring nations? God gave Joseph favor and wisdom with the governing authorities to implement His plan of provision and protection during troubled times. Joseph's (God's) storehouse plan is shown in the first book of the Bible, Genesis:

The Storehouse Plan

So with severe famine everywhere, Joseph opened up the storehouses and distributed grain to the Egyptians, for the famine was severe throughout the land of Egypt. And people from all around came to Egypt to buy grain from Joseph because the famine was severe throughout the world.

(Genesis 41:56-57, NLT)

Joseph (the Church) had plenty of grain to satisfy the starving people. He (The Church) distributed it to those who had need. Joseph was looked upon as a great man, not only in the land of Egypt but in the lands beyond Egyptian borders.

As the Church seeks to fulfill her role in these end times to offer the only hope there is—Jesus Christ—

and to be a witness of God's goodness and blessing, to God be the glory!

To get started, begin to pray and seek God's direction for your church if you are a pastor or other church leader. You will find more specific details, plus a model of an existing local church food ministry that is operating successfully and blessing many in its community, in chapter seven *Especially for Pastors: A Message and Model.* If you are not a pastor or church leader, you might want to consider providing a copy of this book to your church leaders.

Each church could set up a "needs committee" to determine the following:

A. The needs of the community for food and basic necessities

B. The current resources of the church (and other nearby churches)

C. How existing resources can be expanded or new resources developed

D. The best approach to get congregation members involved

A good idea is to talk with other Christian churches that already have such an outreach ministry in place. Enlist their advice and help. Join in their efforts; several churches can get together to develop a community outreach that will be more effective than the operation of a lone church.

You can also contact my ministry, Jesus Healing House Ministries (more information in chapter six *Miracles Still*

Happen: "Fear Not and Only Believe"), for organizational assistance.

Miracles of supernatural provision

God will supernaturally provide for His people in such abundance that we will be able to reach out to a world that desperately needs Jesus. I think this is what the prosperity movement is all about—not to accumulate excessive wealth to use for oneself lavishly, but to be prepared to be a blessing to the masses in the end times, and to bring glory to God. This will accomplish:

(1) A "where the rubber meets the road" demonstration of God's love and caring.

(2) Multitudes of people hearing about Jesus Christ, believing, repenting and entering the kingdom of God. Romans 2:4 tells us that "the goodness of God leads people to repentance."

(3) As the world sees how God provides for those who trust in Him through ways that exceed the limitations of the world's economic and political system, many people will be drawn to this God of love, power and supernatural provision.

Trust (lean on, rely on, and be confident) in the Lord and do good; so shall you dwell in the land and feed surely on His faithfulness, and truly you shall be fed.

(Psalm 37:3, AMP)

"Ho! Everyone who thirsts, Come to the waters; And you who have no money, Come, buy and eat. Yes, come, buy wine and milk Without money and without price."

(Isaiah 55:1, NKJV)

Seek the Kingdom of God above all else, and live righteously, and he will give you everything you need.

(Matthew 6:33, NLT)

Then He took the five loaves and the two fish, and looking up to heaven He blessed and broke them and gave them to the disciples to set before the multitude. So they all ate and were filled...

(Luke 9:16-17, NKJV)

Brothers and sisters, remember that our churches will only be able to do as much as we allow God to do through US. Today, many churches who give out food get that food from government sources. Praise God for that provision now, but the times I am talking about will be different. I believe the government will come to the Church for help, not the Church going to the government for help. God intends for the Church to be not only self-sufficient (through His miraculous and abundant provision), but to have enough to help others. What an exciting time to witness about God's love and power!

Churches are joining together to make a difference in their communities

The "Community Storehouse," a wonderful community outreach in a little town in North Texas, is a phenomenal ecumenical effort by several churches to stock a community location with food and other basic necessities for giving out to those in need. They also offer job assistance and various other services. What a great example of churches getting together and laying aside doctrinal differences and self-focused agendas to serve Christ and the precious souls He loves!

Another church a few towns away from the "Community Storehouse," also has a food distribution center along with a temporary residence for single moms and their children who need help. In addition, this center also combines these two outreaches with a prayer center.

Another church has set up an "Emergency Response Team" to go out to various locations in the United States that are hit by earthquakes, floods, or other emergency situations and help the citizens that have been affected. They provide food, clothing and other material needs, spiritual counsel and hope, and most of all the love of Jesus.

Multiple other churches in this state and many other states offer food distribution, clothing, job assistance, prayer and Bible teaching to help people not only with their immediate needs but to become self-sufficient for the future. The days will come when we don't have to travel to another city or state, but will have the opportunity to serve in our own backyards.

Outreaches such as these have long been a service of practical love shown by many churches. In the Bible, Jesus says,

> *35 for I was hungry and you gave Me food; I was thirsty and you gave Me drink; I was a stranger and you took Me in;*
>
> *36 I was naked and you clothed Me; I was sick and you visited Me; I was in prison and you came to Me.'*
>
> *37 "Then the righteous will answer Him, saying, 'Lord, when did we see You hungry and feed You, or thirsty and give You drink?*
>
> *38 When did we see You a stranger and take You in, or naked and clothe You?*
>
> *39 Or when did we see You sick, or in prison, and come to You?'*
>
> *40 And the King will answer and say to them, 'Assuredly, I say to you, inasmuch as you did it to one of the least of these My brethren, you did it to Me.'*
>
> (Matthew 25:35-40, NKJV)

What a great example not only of Christian love toward hurting people, but this model demonstrates what true Christianity is all about.

Your love for one another will prove to the world that you are my disciples."

(John 13:35, NLT)

Most of these church-run ministries and organizations are manned with a small paid staff, and a larger number of volunteers from within their own congregations or combined with members of like-minded churches.

In these tumultuous times, the Church must take her place not just spiritually, but in practical assistance toward the community. In days of food shortages, job losses, and desperation, the Church can literally be a life-saving instrument of God's love and provision.

How can I help myself, my family, and help others, too?

Dear Reader…Whether or not your church participates in a community outreach such as this, you as an individual believer and your family can take steps to help yourself and others. Here are a few very practical, personal ideas: Practical steps you can take now to prepare, including accumulating supplies not only for yourself, but also for others in the surrounding community.

o   Be economical. Cut out waste. Ask God to show you what, where and how.

o   In my house, we are beginning to take measures such as storing imperishable food, basic necessities, not feeding our puppy $1 per tiny cup of gourmet dog food, but a middle-grade dog food; using each food dollar to purchase healthy foods rather than "junk" foods that cannot sustain health, also for ingredients that will stretch farther to make meals, and sharing what we have with others, too. One of my favorite things to store is a protein powder which stays good just about forever, is full of nutrients, and mixes easily with reconstituted powdered milk, soy milk or rice milk. You can best store the brands that don't require refrigeration.

o   Cut down on entertainment and eating out.

o   Buy a smaller car that gets greater gas economy or carpool when possible.

o   Wait to do the laundry until you have a full load.

o   Celebrate holidays less expensively; cut down on "consumerism" and find creative ways to bless others…especially your children; they'll enjoy the time you spend together as a family more than expensive toys.

o   Wear the clothes you already have instead of buying new ones.

o   Reduce the number and frequency of extracurricular activities; spend more family time together instead. Play board games or have a movie night at home with popcorn from the microwave.

o   Have heart-to-heart talks about what really matters. Tell your husband or wife, son or daughter, or other loved one, how great you think they are. Say, "I love you." And "I'm sorry for those times, I… (fill in the blank)" o Home gardening: Maybe your thing is gardening? You can plant a garden at home, either inside or outside depending on the season of the year. You can teach others how to do the same. Check for health and gardening tips on the Internet.

o PRAY, and ask God to reveal any other areas of waste in your life that you can eliminate. This is always a good idea during good and bad times!

I have focused mostly on practical suggestions in this chapter, but the foundation of spiritual principles is even more important as keys of survival in the closing days of this age.

Miracles of the God-kind

I believe that we are about to see a display of the supernatural power of God in miracles, signs and wonders like we've never seen before! Not only in the miraculous provision of food, divine direction, and protection for believers in these end times, but we will also witness miracles in the area of supernatural healing and deliverance.

There will be plagues that doctors are unable to cure. Healthcare systems may become unaffordable or fail altogether. National healthcare is not the answer either. Consider this story I heard about a lady in the U.K. where national health insurance is in operation: "I woke up with pain so great, I had to call an ambulance to take me to the hospital. The doctors found a tumor in my stomach the size of a large orange. But, they sent me home, treated only with pain medication because they wouldn't be able to do surgery for three months." This lady was later healed miraculously—praise God! However, the point here is that a government health system leads to delays, corruption, incompetence, and an increased tax burden on its citizens.

(Please see more in chapter six *Miracles Still Happen: Fear Not and Only Believe* to help you build a solid spiritual foundation for supernatural living and God's miraculous provision.

Church...Are you willing? Are you ready?

Church, God has set before you an open door that no man can shut (Rev. 3:8) through the persecution and need that is rising up in America. Many people are becoming aware through the abundance of movies, books and Internet blogs they are seeing pop up everywhere and are beginning to question if truly we are in the end times. What a great open door lies before the Church...an open door to share the Gospel of Jesus Christ through the renewed awakening of men's spirits, the tenderness of heart that comes during troubled times, and the demonstration of God's goodness in meeting their desperate needs.

Will you enter in this open door?

Chapter Five

Destruction from Within the Church: Differences, Divisions, and Divine Direction!

Strife causes destruction from within. A church, house, workplace, city, nation, or a relationship cannot survive when there is division and strife in its midst. The place of strife will become ineffective and counter-productive. Confusion will reign; deception will take charge, and the people who are involved will lose much: reputation, honor, relationships, finances or material possessions, position, possibly even their lives. What a price to pay for "being right," or "winning an argument," or "having your own way!"

> *And knowing their thoughts, (Jesus) said to them, Any kingdom that is divided against itself is being brought to desolation and laid waste, and no city or house divided against itself will last or continue to stand.*

> (Matthew 12:25, AMP)

Remember the sad predicament of the Civil War in America, where brother fought brother and neighboring states fought each other? The blood of one American was at the hand of another American. What a heartbreaking moment in American history for all of us in this country. So much was lost, and what was gained should have been possible to attain without war.

Brother fighting brother didn't start in 1861 when the war between the states broke out. This deadly act of violence has its roots in a time and place that existed a long time before then. We see brother fighting brother at the beginning of God's creation, when Cain was jealous because his brother's gift was more pleasing and acceptable to God than his was. Though Cain had an opportunity to change the situation, what did he choose to do? Murder! He killed his brother, Abel!

Jesus Forbids Sectarianism

Of course, brother fighting brother can occur on a much less obvious level that doesn't result in physical death, but in ways that divide people, hinder the Gospel, and cause hurt and confusion. I think the worst outcome is how division within the body of Christ drives unbelievers further from the truth of the Gospel, giving them an excuse for "not being like those Christians when all they do is attack one another."

Where is Christian love?

Your love for one another will prove to the
world that you are my disciples."

(John 13:35, NLT)

Sometimes, well-intentioned and sincere Christians see a brother or sister, or another church, that differs in doctrine from their own and judge it to be "false" or not of God. Of course, we must always agree on the basics of the Gospel: Jesus' crucifixion, resurrection and coming again. There is no disputing that anything which disagrees with the core doctrines of the Christian faith should be rejected.

However, one of the truths in God's Word that comes under fire today is that miracles have passed away. In the following Scripture, Jesus shows that others should not be judged as false because they are not necessarily from your own group or teach exactly the same as you do.

38 Now John answered Him, saying, "Teacher, we saw someone who does not follow us casting out demons in Your name, and we forbade him because he does not follow us."

39 But Jesus said, "Do not forbid him, for no one who works a miracle in My name can soon afterward speak evil of Me.

40 For he who is not against us is on our side.

41 For whoever gives you a cup of water to drink in My name, because you belong to Christ, assuredly, I say to you, he will by no means lose his reward.

(Mark 9:38-41, NKJV)

As you read the next chapter, you will find much about Jesus' miracles, and how we will need to believe and accept God's miraculous works and provisions if we are to survive in spite of the persecution that runs rampant in today's world view. Of course, many Christians will be martyred for their faith, which brings great reward, but for others I believe God will make a way of escape! However, you'll have to be open to ways which may not be the norm that we are used to expecting.

Stand with your brother, not against him.

Christian, do not stand or side with this unbelieving, atheistic world that condemns and mocks the works and people of God! Trust God to separate the "chaff" from the wheat, and just love and accept your fellow believers who honor and preach our Lord Jesus Christ.

It doesn't matter if we speak in "tongues" or if we don't speak in tongues. This is a wonderful gift from God that helps the believer to "pray in the spirit" without the limitation of their human understanding getting in the way, but it's not mandatory for salvation. Speaking or not speaking in tongues, operating or not operating in the gifts of the Spirit is not the deciding criteria as to whether one is a true Christian and has inherited the promise of eternal life in heaven with God.

So, my precious brother and sister in Christ, do not judge those who speak in tongues or operate in the spiritual gifts of Corinthians 12, and those who do—do not judge those who don't. We must put aside these petty disagreements and concentrate our efforts on that which will determine whether a person goes to heaven or hell when they die—the Gospel of Jesus Christ.

Instead of judging each other, let's pray for each other—and with each other—for a world that needs to see love at work!

We are looking at times where history will be repeated, but on a broader, more technologically advanced scale. History tells us that in the early Church in the time of Nero and other ruthless rulers, Christians were crucified, thrown to wild beasts, and burned to death for their refusal to worship the emperor and deny their faith in Jesus Christ. You may be wrestling in your mind with self-searching questions like…

- o Am I really ready to meet Jesus? Will God accept me?
- o Will I be able to endure this kind of persecution and still stay strong for my Lord?
- o Or, will I renounce Jesus like Peter did in the face of fear?

God's presence inhabits our praise!

Thank God for how He has taken care of you in the past. Thank God for what you have now. Thank God that He will continue to take care of you. Sing songs about God's goodness and glory. Find a church hymnal or songbook, or speak words from the book of Psalms in the Bible out loud. These are filled with inspiring praises to God from King

David, who God said was a "man after His own heart." What an awesome declaration of David's faithfulness in spite of his imperfections and failures!

God is looking for people to worship Him in spirit and in truth.

> *A time will come, however, indeed it is already here, when the true (genuine) worshipers will worship the Father in spirit and in truth (reality); for the Father is seeking just such people as these as His worshipers.*
>
> (John 4:23, AMP)

Jesus said it will no longer be a matter of where we worship, what traditions or rituals we follow, or a whole group of other things that matter to churches and denominations, but not to God. He wants us to worship by the power of the Holy Spirit and according to knowledge of the Scriptures. God wants us to get real with Him, and worship with our hearts, not just with our lips.

> *"'These people honor me with their lips, but their hearts are far from me. They worship me in vain; their teachings are but rules taught by men.'"*
>
> (Matthew 15:8-9, NIV)

My brother and sister in the Lord, let us all examine our hearts before God to see if we have been guilty of judging our brother, or of worship that isn't truly in "spirit and truth" …just going through the motions, going to church, praying, reading our Bibles out of duty but not with the real joy we should experience in an intimate relationship with Jesus.

Praising God brings salvation and freedom!

Paul and Silas had set a slave girl free from a demon! Her owners, who had now lost their profitability because she no longer could tell fortunes, as well as the angry townspeople, were anything but happy about this. They dragged Paul and Silas before the authorities. Let's pick up the Scripture from here:

22 A mob quickly formed against Paul and Silas, and the city officials ordered them stripped and beaten with wooden rods.

23 They were severely beaten, and then they were thrown into prison. The jailer was ordered to make sure they didn't escape.

24 So the jailer put them into the inner dungeon and clamped their feet in the stocks.

25 Around midnight Paul and Silas were praying and singing hymns to God, and the other prisoners were listening.

26 Suddenly, there was a massive earthquake, and the prison was shaken to its foundations. All the doors immediately flew open, and the chains of every prisoner fell off!

27 The jailer woke up to see the prison doors wide open. He assumed the prisoners had escaped, so he drew his sword to kill himself.

28 But Paul shouted to him, "Stop! Don't kill yourself! We are all here!"

29 The jailer called for lights and ran to the dungeon and fell down trembling before Paul and Silas.

30 Then he brought them out and asked, "Sirs, what must I do to be saved?"

31 They replied, "Believe in the Lord Jesus and you will be saved, along with everyone in your household."

32 And they shared the word of the Lord with him and with all who lived in his household.

33 Even at that hour of the night, the jailer cared for them and washed their wounds. Then he and everyone in his household were immediately baptized.

34 He brought them into his house and set a meal before them, and he and his entire household rejoiced because they all believed in God.

35 The next morning the city officials sent the police to tell the jailer, "Let those men go!"

36 So the jailer told Paul, "The city officials have said you and Silas are free to leave. Go in peace."

(Acts 16-22-36, NLT)

Were Paul and Silas trembling in fear and anger, desiring to retaliate for the suffering they had just wrongfully experienced? No! Instead, they were praying and singing praises to God! There are several points worth mentioning here:

- o Prayer and praise kept Paul and Silas strong in their faith.
- o Their attitudes and actions witnessed to others about the goodness and power of God.
- o As a result, God sent a powerful earthquake to open the prison doors and set Paul and Silas free from their chains and captivity!
- o All of the prisoners were also delivered, though they willingly chose to remain in the prison because it would have meant certain death for the jailor if the prisoners had escaped on his watch.
- o Seeing this, the jailor and his family believed in Jesus and were saved!

Hear what the Spirit is saying to the Church

My fellow believer, open your heart to hear what God's Spirit is saying to the Church today, and what He is saying to you. In the first three chapters of the book of Revelation, God imparts a message to the churches of that day, which are indicative of the condition in the churches today, and in the lives of individual believers.

Return to your first love

To the first church (Ephesus), God expressed approval over their labor, patience and solid stand on integrity, but He warned them against the following danger:

2 "I know all the things you do. I have seen your hard work and your patient endurance. I know you don't tolerate evil people. You have examined the claims of those who say they are apostles but are not. You have discovered they are liars.

3 You have patiently suffered for me without quitting.

4 "But I have this complaint against you. You don't love me or each other as you did at first

5 Look how far you have fallen! Turn back to me and do the works you did at first. If you don't repent, I will come and remove your lampstand from its place among the churches."

(Revelation 2:2-5, NLT)

They had lost their "first love" Jesus Christ.

Do you remember when you first became "born again" by the Spirit of God? It was like a honeymoon—just you and the Lord. You awoke with thoughts of Jesus…you endeavored to live in a way that was pleasing to Him, honoring to Him. Many of the things that were important to you before just didn't seem all that necessary anymore; you just wanted to spend time with your new-found Love!

Without a passionate love for Jesus—and for others— our works become useless. Materialism (the love of and excessive accumulation of things), becoming too busy, and worrying about the cares of life are prime contributors to the loss of fervency and sincerity in our love for Christ.

Repent now and say, "Lord Jesus, restore to me my "first love" for you. Help me to spend quality time with you, adoring you, and sharing my innermost feelings with you."

Are you a Martha or a Mary?

Though the "Marthas" of this world (the doers, the achievers) are to be admired and may accomplish much good; it is really the "Marys" who achieve the greater success at least in the spiritual arena, which lasts for eternity, not just a brief time here on earth.

> *38 As Jesus and his disciples were on their way, he came to a village where a woman named Martha opened her home to him.*
>
> *39 She had a sister called Mary, who sat at the Lord's feet listening to what he said.*
>
> *40 But Martha was distracted by all the preparations that had to be made. She came to him and asked, "Lord, don't you care that my sister has left me to do the work by myself? Tell her to help me!"*
>
> *41 "Martha, Martha," the Lord answered, "you are worried and upset about many things,*
>
> *42 but only one thing is needed. Mary has chosen what is better, and it will not be taken away from her."*

(Luke 10:38-42, NIV)

Do not fear the things to come

To the second church (Smyrna), the Lord again commended their good works as well as their loyalty for Him in spite of suffering severe persecution. But, Jesus warned them not to fear the things that were coming upon the earth...the trials they were going through...because He would be with them.

> *"Don't be afraid of what you are about to suffer. The devil will throw some of you into prison to test you. You will suffer for ten days. But if you remain faithful even when facing death, I will give you the crown of life."*
>
> (Revelation 2:10, NLT)

In America, so far, we have been greatly blessed with freedom to worship God and conduct religious services and practices. In other countries, such as Asia, believers in underground churches suffer beatings, imprisonment and death for their unyielding commitment to Jesus Christ. In Muslim nations, people who convert from Islam are beaten; they lose their families, jobs and homes as a result of their faith in Jesus.

The day may come in America when our religious liberties are stripped from us and Christians become "the enemy" in the mindset of mainstream society. Don't say it can't happen here—it can if we don't continue to be watchful in prayer and seek to turn America back to God.

Fear of dying

Because God's children are human beings—made of flesh and blood—the Son also became flesh and blood. For only as a human being could he die, and only by dying could he break the power of the devil, who had the power of death. Only in this way could he set free all who have lived their lives as slaves to the fear of dying.

(Hebrews 2:14-15, NLT)

Perfect love casts out fear

Scripture tells us that "perfect" love casts out all fear. This is a love that transcends human love, which is frail and conditional. Perfect love is a love that is poured into our hearts by God's Spirit; it is not something we possess naturally or can conjure up in ourselves.

There is no fear in love; but perfect love casts out fear...

(1 John 4:18, NKJV)

God gave me a hard illustration of perfect love casting out fear, which is this: Imagine for a moment that we are truly in the end of the last days and that you are being persecuted for your faith in Jesus Christ. Imagine that you have been arrested, or worse, that you are being beaten or tortured in an effort to get you to renounce Christ. Imagine the most horrible type of abuse you can picture in your mind. (This is really hard, I know, but there is a point here.)

Then, imagine that God is pouring His "perfect love" in your heart. Look at your persecutor—straight in the eye if possible—with that love of God. Know that God loves him just as much as He loves you. This persecutor is somebody's son or daughter…somebody's brother or sister…somebody's mom or dad who has been deceived into thinking that he or she is in the right and that we are the enemy. "Feel" that love of God welling up inside you for that persecutor who is causing you great pain. You will find that you no longer fear him, but instead the very compassion of Christ will flood your soul.

Impossible? You say, "I could never love someone who is torturing me!"

Does Christ live inside of you? Is He your example? Then, it is possible for you to have this kind of love that will set you free from fear. Why? Because this is the very same thing Christ did on the cross when He said, "Father, forgive them because they do not know what they are doing." Furthermore, Jesus Christ did this for you and me…when we were yet full of sin, He died for us, having a love that was perfect, in spite of our own imperfections.

Jesus has called us to be "perfect" as He is perfect… to walk in the same kind of love that He did. But, do not fear, my dear brother and sister. You cannot possibly have that kind of perfect love inside of you by your own human decision or efforts to make it happen. It will take a divine deposit of Christ's own Spirit in you…all that He asks is that you be willing to receive it.

Say with me today to your Lord and my Lord, "Yes, Lord, I am willing to love as You love. Fill me with your compassion and unconditional love for others this day, even those who may hurt me."

> *When He had called the people to Himself,*
> *with His disciples also, He said to them,*
> *"Whoever desires to come after Me, let him*
> *deny himself, and take up his cross, and follow*
> *Me. For whoever desires to save his life will*
> *lose it, but whoever loses his life for My sake*
> *and the gospel's will save it.*
>
> (Mark 8:34-35, NKJV)

Make the main thing the main thing!

Friends, it is time to set aside our petty judgments of each other, our doctrinal differences and make the main thing the main thing: Jesus Christ and Himself crucified. John the Baptist and then Jesus preached, "Repent for the kingdom of God is at hand." Never has there been a day when that is more true than now! We are at the very threshold of Christ's return, and must devote all of our energies and efforts to being ready…and making sure that others are ready too. (Please see more about this in chapter nine: *Departing for Heaven at "Gate Jesus": Don't Miss Your Departure Time!)*

We need to STOP criticizing each other…we need to

STOP condemning each other...we need to STOP pointing out the faults and downfalls of others. It is time to stand together in faith in Jesus Christ. Let us be ashamed in the Body of Christ of how we have behaved before the world. Is it any wonder they don't want any part of Christianity when they see the criticism and infighting in the Church?

We don't have to agree on every point of doctrinal belief as long as we agree on the major points of the Christian faith: God's love, grace and mercy shown through the life, crucifixion, death, burial and resurrection of our Lord Jesus Christ. We agree that the world is filled with people who are on their way to hell, and if we, as Christian believers, don't stop fighting each other and start fighting the devil over the souls of these people, telling them the Way, the Truth and the Life is Jesus Christ, their blood will be on our hands.

Turn from hypocrisy and compromise

Church number three (Pergamos) was also commended for their good works and for their perseverance in not denying their faith, but they too received a severe warning from the Lord. This church had gotten off into error, coupled with hypocrisy and compromise, leading them into spiritual destruction. They had become indifferent toward sin, and in their efforts to fit in with the world, they no longer preached a pure Gospel.

> *13 "I know that you live in the city where Satan has his throne, yet you have remained loyal to me. You refused to deny me even when*

Antipas, my faithful witness, was martyred among you there in Satan's city.

14 "But I have a few complaints against you. You tolerate some among you whose teaching is like that of Balaam, who showed Balak how to trip up the people of Israel. He taught them to sin by eating food offered to idols and by committing sexual sin.

15 In a similar way, you have some Nicolaitans among you who follow the same teaching.

16 Repent of your sin, or I will come to you suddenly and fight against them with the sword of my mouth."

(Revelation 2:13-16. NLT)

Judgment in the Church

The fourth church (Thyatira) was commended for their works, charity, service, faith and patience. But, they allowed moral compromise to run rampant in the church.

Just like this church, look at America's history—sin, decay and destruction increase with each new generation. Escalating crime, divorce, and our "anything goes" lifestyles have skyrocketed into epidemics of disease, broken families, an overwhelming suicide rate, depression and utter hopelessness. Idolatry and rebellion toward God, characterized by self-pride, results in an attitude of independence apart from God. "I'll do it my way," boasts the famous song crooned by Frank Sinatra, but unfortunately "my way" when it is contrary to God's ways usually turns out to be disastrous.

> *19 "I know all the things you do. I have seen your love, your faith, your service, and your patient endurance. And I can see your constant improvement in all these things.*
>
> *20 "But I have this complaint against you. You are permitting that woman—that Jezebel who calls herself a prophet—to lead my servants astray. She teaches them to commit sexual sin and to eat food offered to idols.*
>
> *21 I gave her time to repent, but she does not want to turn away from her immorality.*
>
> *22 "Therefore, I will throw her on a bed of suffering, and those who commit adultery with her will suffer greatly unless they repent and turn away from her evil deeds.*
>
> *23 I will strike her children dead. Then all the churches will know that I am the one who searches out the thoughts and intentions of every person. And I will give to each of you whatever you deserve."*
>
> (Revelation 2: 19-23, NLT)

Idols are anything in our lives that become more important that the Creator of life. These include excessive material possessions, recreation and entertainment, idols of career and selfish ambition, and anything else that makes you forget God or gives Him a backseat to your other interests. Many believers today have areas in their lives where they have refused to surrender to the Lordship of Jesus Christ.

Friend, ask Jesus today to reveal anything in your life that is taking His place in your heart. Then repent of whatever He shows you, and be restored in your fellowship with God. We may think God is taking good things away from us, but that is not so; He is really just freeing us up so that we can receive His better things…His better way. You will be glad He did!

Be watchful and hold fast the things of God

Church number five (Sardis) appeared to have a good reputation and to be a productive church, but inwardly, Jesus said they were "dead." He warned this church that if they did not repent and hold fast to the sound teaching they had received, He (Jesus) would come as unexpectedly as a thief in the night. These believers would be unprepared and not ready for Jesus' return.

> *"…I know your works, that you have a name that you are alive, but you are dead. Be watchful, and strengthen the things which remain, that are ready to die, for I have not found your works perfect before God Remember therefore how you have received and heard; hold fast and repent. Therefore if you will not watch, I will come upon you as a thief, and you will not know what hour I will come upon you."*
>
> (Revelation 3:1-3, NLT)

God opens the door that no man can shut

The sixth church (Philadelphia) was approved by the Lord without any warnings. Notice the name of this church: Philadelphia, which means "brotherly love." Love for others is a major foundation if you want to be right with God and ready for Jesus' return. Because this is such a vital church, and is symbolic of the age we are now living in, I am showing the entire, related Scripture here:

> 7 *"Write this letter to the angel of the church in Philadelphia. This is the message from the one who is holy and true, the one who has the key of David. What he opens, no one can close; and what he closes, no one can open:*

> 8 *"I know all the things you do, and I have opened a door for you that no one can close. You have little strength, yet you obeyed my word and did not deny me.*

> 9 *Look, I will force those who belong to Satan's synagogue—those liars who say they are Jews but are not—to come and bow down at your feet. They will acknowledge that you are the ones I love.*

> 10 *"Because you have obeyed my command to persevere, I will protect you from the great time of testing that will come upon the whole world to test those who belong to this world.*

> 11 *I am coming soon. Hold on to what you have, so that no one will take away your crown.*

*12 All who are victorious will become pillars
in the Temple of my God, and they will never
have to leave it. And I will write on them the
name of my God, and they will be citizens in
the city of my God—the new Jerusalem that
comes down from heaven from my God. And I
will also write on them my new name.*

*13 "Anyone with ears to hear must listen to
the Spirit and understand what he is saying to
the churches."*

(Revelation 3:7-13, NLT)

In this encouraging text, we see several things that
God will do for those who believe and overcome… who
persevere in their faith, and are alert and actively serving
God in this time:

o   God will shut the wrong doors in our lives.
o   God will open the right doors that no man can
    shut.
o   God will overcome our enemies.
o   God will keep us from the tribulation.
o   God will give us a heavenly crown.

Notice also that Jesus said that these believers had a
"little strength." Isn't it encouraging to know that we do
not have to be supermen and wonder women, but just to be
faithful with what we have, and God will do the rest! It is
His power in us and His promise never to leave or forsake
us that will see us through any situation (Hebrews 13:5).
Praise the Lord!

The church at Philadelphia is a picture of the true believers who are eagerly waiting for the entrance of their King, Jesus Christ, and to reign with Him in heaven and on earth forever and ever. These children of God are sharing the Gospel to bring others into God's kingdom while there is still time and freedom to do it.

The church that didn't need God

The seventh and final church (Laodicea) that Jesus addressed in the book of Revelation is also alive and flourishing today. But of this church, Jesus didn't have nearly as many good things to say as He did about Philadelphia. Because this church too is of vital importance, and we need to understand and beware of the pitfalls these believers found themselves in, I am showing the related Scripture in its entirety:

> *14 "Write this letter to the angel of the church in Laodicea. This is the message from the one who is the Amen—the faithful and true witness, the beginning of God's new creation:*
>
> *15 "I know all the things you do, that you are neither hot nor cold. I wish that you were one or the other!*
>
> *16 But since you are like lukewarm water, neither hot nor cold, I will spit you out of my mouth!*
>
> *17 You say, 'I am rich. I have everything I want. I don't need a thing!' And you don't realize that you are wretched and miserable and poor and blind and naked.*

18 So I advise you to buy gold from me—gold that has been purified by fire. Then you will be rich. Also buy white garments from me so you will not be shamed by your nakedness, and ointment for your eyes so you will be able to see."

(Revelation 3:14-18, NLT)

The believers in the church of Laodicea were not totally cold toward Christ, but neither were they hot—fervent in their love and service toward the King of Kings and the Lord of Lords. Jesus called them "lukewarm." This so angered God that He declared, "Because you are lukewarm, and neither cold nor hot, I will spue you out of My mouth." He wanted to spit them out! These believers were spiritually blind and naked; they were so filled with goods and riches, they thought they didn't need God.

There is a connection in the Scripture portion above between the Laodiceans' lukewarm attitudes and their preoccupation with riches. Friend, it's time to shake off complacency and materialism!

Hear what the Spirit is saying to the Church!

The hour is critical and the time is short—we must get our focus off of the temporal and temporary things of this earth, off ourselves, our hurts and our needs, and focus on the precious souls for whom Jesus died and the Father longs to bring into His kingdom. Are your family members, your friends, your co-workers, your neighbors saved and ready for eternity? Be sensitive and alert to opportunities to share Christ with them. Pray for an impartation of God's compassion and boldness to rise up in you like it did with Peter and John. How? By spending quality, intimate time with Jesus.

> *Now when they saw the boldness of Peter and John, and perceived that they were uneducated and untrained men, they marveled. And they realized that they had been with Jesus.*

(Acts 4:13, NKJV)

Church, it's time to examine ourselves to see if we have fallen into any of the same spiritual traps and pitfalls that these churches did. It's time also to lay aside our differences and join together in looking up because Jesus is coming soon! He will not be pleased if when He comes, He finds us devoting our time and efforts to attacking each other—those within the Church, our brothers and sisters—instead of being faithful to the great commission He's given us:

> *And Jesus came and spoke to them, saying, "All authority has been given to Me in heaven and on earth. Go therefore and make disciples of all the nations, baptizing them in the name of the Father and of the Son and of the Holy Spirit, teaching them to observe all things that I have commanded you; and lo, I am with you always, even to the end of the age." Amen.*

(Matthew 28:18-20, NKJV)

Chapter Six

Miracles Still Happen: "Fear Not and Only Believe"

Jesus came to earth to save man from sin and restore the relationship between God and man both during our human lifespan on the earth and in heaven for eternity. Jesus' mission was to bring the kingdom of God to earth and ultimately believers to the kingdom of God in heaven. While on earth, Jesus brought not only spiritual salvation, but healing to the sick and freedom to those who were bound, tormented, and hopeless.

> *The Spirit of the Lord is on me, because he has anointed me to preach good news to the poor. He has sent me to proclaim freedom for the prisoners and recovery of sight for the blind, to release the oppressed, to proclaim the year of the Lord's favor."*
>
> (Luke 4:18-19, NIV)

The Bible is not a storybook. It is a divine Operator's manual from the Creator to His creation—you and me. In the Bible, you will find instructions on how to discover and live out God's wonderful plan for your life. You were created by the heavenly Father for a special and unique purpose. His plan for your life is custom-made for you. There is no one else quite like you…no one else who can fulfill God's awesome plan and purpose just for you.

> *For I know the plans I have for you," declares the LORD, "plans to prosper you and not to harm you, plans to give you hope and a future. Then you will call upon me and come and pray to me, and I will listen to you. You will seek me and find me when you seek me with all your heart.*
>
> (Jeremiah 29:11-13, NIV)

The first place to start is by making sure that you have been spiritually "born again." (Please see chapter nine *Departing for Heaven at "Gate Jesus": Don't Miss Your Departure Time!* if you have not yet had this experience.) God's Holy Spirit lives inside of you. To walk in the supernatural provision and miracles of God, you have to learn to walk in the Spirit, not in your natural fleshly understanding and limitations.

"Be it unto you according to your faith."

When Jesus walked the earth, He did many miracles of provision, healing, deliverance and even raising the dead! More often than not, you would hear Him say, "Be it unto you according to your faith."

If I had to choose the TOP principle in kingdom living, I would pick FAITH, without a doubt:

Raise the level of your faith…

o   Refuse to fear or compromise!

o   Refuse to blame others, and walk in love!

o   Refuse to hold back, but move forward in confidence!

Practical, everyday needs meet
the miraculous hand of God!

In both the Old and New Testaments there are many miracles from parting the Red Sea to walking on water. In these troubled times, we will need the kind of faith that moved the prophets and patriarchs of old as well as the followers of Jesus to believe that "all things are possible with God!"

Here are just a few examples straight from the Bible text of the miraculous hand of God meeting the needs of people in a supernatural way that defied the laws of nature and the human comprehension of men:

God did many miracles, signs and wonders to deliver His people from slavery and the torment they were experiencing at the hands of the rulers of Egypt (a symbol signifying the world's system). When the Israelites left the Egyptian captivity, they did not go out empty-handed or weak. God caused their captors to willingly give over their riches into the hands of His people. Even though, the Israelites suffered beatings, little rest, and probably weren't fed with the same affluence that the citizens enjoyed, when God brought them out of Egypt, there was not one weak or sick person. This is supernatural health and healing!

He also brought them out with silver and gold,
And there was none feeble among His tribes.

(Psalm 105:37, NKJV)

A 40-year-long detour through the wilderness

They could have gone directly into the promised land, a land flowing with milk and honey…and every good thing, but The Israelites, because of their disobedience, took a 40-year-long detour through the wilderness. It was a place with nothing—worse than their experience in Egypt, or so some of them bitterly complained. But even here, in this barren place, God fed His people supernaturally with "manna" to eat every day and water to drink from a rock. Later, after more of their complaining, He added quail to their diet.

Then the LORD said to Moses, "Behold, I
will rain bread from heaven for you…"I have
heard the complaints of the children of Israel.
Speak to them, saying, 'At twilight you shall
eat meat (quail), and in the morning you shall
be filled with bread. And you shall know that I
am the LORD your God.'" And the children of
Israel ate manna forty years…

(Exodus 16:4, 12, 35, NKJV)

Not only did God provide silver and gold, health and strength, food and water in a place where there was nothing, God supernaturally sustained even their clothes and shoes!

*And I have led you forty years in the
wilderness. Your clothes have not worn out on
you, and your sandals have not worn out on
your feet.*

(Deuteronomy 29:5, NKJV)

Can you imagine wearing your same clothes and shoes for 40 years, without them ever wearing out?

The Israelites, like some of us today, got angry and complained when things didn't go their way or the food God provided for them to eat wasn't exactly lobster and filet mignon in the desert. You may be reading this at any time of the year, but as I am writing this book; it is just a few days before Thanksgiving Day. I am reminded of the proverb which teaches that a piece of plain food eaten in peace is better and more enjoyable than a gourmet meal eaten where there is strife (complaining and arguing). Thankfulness toward God will make even the simplest meal or other provision a reason to rejoice!

Embarking on a journey of faith

Abraham is considered, the "father of faith." He lived by faith continually, and his faith was considered unto him as righteousness by God, who had not yet sent the promised Messiah. Abraham set out by faith, not knowing where he was going, when God told him to leave his family and all that he knew for a place that He would show him. God promised Abraham and his wife Sarah, who were childless in their latter years, that she would bear him a child and he

169

would be the "father of nations." God also told Abraham that the number of his descendants would be as many as the stars in the sky. God enabled Abraham at over 100 years old to impregnate his wife Sarah, who at age 90, was able to conceive and deliver a baby son, whom they named Isaac.

> *1 Now the LORD was gracious to Sarah as he had said, and the LORD did for Sarah what he had promised.*
>
> *2 Sarah became pregnant and bore a son to Abraham in his old age, at the very time God had promised him.*
>
> *3 Abraham gave the name Isaac to the son Sarah bore him.*
>
> *4 When his son Isaac was eight days old, Abraham circumcised him, as God commanded him.*
>
> *5 Abraham was a hundred years old when his son Isaac was born to him.*
>
> *6 Sarah said, "God has brought me laughter, and everyone who hears about this will laugh with me."*
>
> *7 And she added, "Who would have said to Abraham that Sarah would nurse children? Yet I have borne him a son in his old age."*
>
> (Genesis 21:1-7, NIV)

Surely, some of you may remember first hearing these stories as a child in Sunday School, along with many more such as how the young shepherd David slew the ferocious giant Goliath and became king, how Queen Esther saved her people from certain annihilation, how Samson fell prey to a wicked woman, and how Daniel survived a night in the lions' den. As amazing as these Old Testament stories are, they were just a shadow of that which was to come.

All of these heroes were faithful servants of the living God, but then God sent His own Son to the earth to do a mighty work far beyond anything that had ever been done before. Jesus preached the kingdom of God. He taught the higher ways of God. And, He demonstrated the love and compassion of God through the incredible miracles He performed in the lives of anyone who would believe He was the Son of God!

Jesus healed the sick and set the captives free everywhere He traveled.

How God anointed and consecrated Jesus of Nazareth with the [Holy] Spirit and with strength and ability and power; how He went about doing good and, in particular, curing all who were harassed and oppressed by [the power of] the devil, for God was with Him.

(Acts 10:38, AMP)

A Blind Man Healed

One of these miraculous instances of healing cured a man who was blind, so that he could see again. Most often, when Jesus ministered to the sick, healing took

171

place immediately, but notice in the following example that in this particular case, the man's full healing came in degrees. He was first partially healed, then completely restored. The thing we need to remember here is that if you are asking God for a healing, or you are praying for the sick, do not become discouraged if you do not see instant results. Keep praying and believing for your miracle. We don't know why the man wasn't fully healed the first time Jesus prayed—it could have been something to do with his faith or sin, or any number of hindrances to healing (unforgiveness, bitterness, fear, unbelief, etc.). We are not told the reason but the important thing is that the man's sight was restored!

> *22 Then He came to Bethsaida; and they brought a blind man to Him, and begged Him to touch him.*
>
> *23 So He took the blind man by the hand and led him out of the town. And when He had spit on his eyes and put His hands on him, He asked him if he saw anything.*
>
> *24 And he looked up and said, "I see men like trees, walking."*
>
> *25 Then He put His hands on his eyes again and made him look up. And he was restored and saw everyone clearly.*
>
> (Mark 8:22-25, NKJV)

Unbelief is a major hindrance to healing

We know that with man, things sometimes go awry. For instance, the time when Jesus' disciples prayed for a young man, oppressed by demons, which caused him to go into horrible seizures. The boy wasn't healed and his father complained to Jesus about why the disciples couldn't heal him. Jesus reprimanded the disciples for their lack of faith and immediately turning to the young man, called the devils out of him. The boy was completely restored and returned to his father whole! (Mark 9:17-29)

If you look up this example in the Bible, you will find that the disciples were not the only ones who were weak in their faith. The father of the boy also had to overcome unbelief: Note the statement I have underlined. This a statement of wishful hope, but at this point you can tell the father thought Jesus "might" be able to help, but wasn't sure. My friend, when you are asking God for your healing or praying for others, you must have steadfast, unshakeable faith that Jesus heals today just like He did in Bible times.

> *21 So He* (Jesus) *asked his father, "How long has this been happening to him?"*
> *And he said, "From childhood.*
>
> *22 And often he has thrown him both into the fire and into the water to destroy him. <u>But if You can do anything, have compassion on us and help us."</u>* (Underlines have been added for emphasis and explanation.)

23 Jesus said to him, "If you can believe, all things are possible to him who believes."

24 Immediately the father of the child cried out and said with tears, "Lord, I believe; help my unbelief!"

(Mark 9:21-24, NKJV)

It is God's Will to Heal You!

Do you remember the story about the leper? He came to Jesus timidly, wondering if Jesus would heal such an outcast as he because lepers weren't even allowed in normal society. It would be similar to being quarantined today with a seriously contagious disease. Yet the man was bold in his faith believing that Jesus could heal him, make him clean (physically and socially), set him free from this dreaded disease, and even recreate body parts to replace those that had been eaten away by the leprosy. But, his hesitancy arose because he wasn't sure if Jesus would want to heal him. Oh, but look at the compassion of Jesus:

Suddenly, a man with leprosy approached him and knelt before him. "Lord," the man said, "if you are willing, you can heal me and make me clean." Jesus reached out and touched him. "I am willing," he said. "Be healed!" And instantly the leprosy disappeared.

(Matthew 8:2-3, NLT)

Five bread and two fishes multiplied to feed thousands

As was customary, Jesus compassionately reached out to the crowds of people following Him. He taught them about the kingdom of God and healed those who were sick. As evening grew near and everyone started getting hungry, Jesus performed one of his greatest miracles! He fed over 5,000 men and an untold number of women and children with only five loaves of bread and two fishes. Do not fear… Jesus will do as much for you when you are wondering, "Where am I going to get enough food for my family?"

12 Late in the afternoon the twelve disciples came to him and said, "Send the crowds away to the nearby villages and farms, so they can find food and lodging for the night. There is nothing to eat here in this remote place."

13 But Jesus said, "You feed them." "But we have only five loaves of bread and two fish," they answered. "Or are you expecting us to go and buy enough food for this whole crowd?"

14 For there were about 5,000 men there. Jesus replied, "Tell them to sit down in groups of about fifty each."

15 So the people all sat down.

16 Jesus took the five loaves and two fish, looked up toward heaven, and blessed them. Then, breaking the loaves into pieces, he kept giving the bread and fish to the disciples so they could distribute it to the people.

17 They all ate as much as they wanted, and afterward, the disciples picked up twelve baskets of leftovers!

(Luke 9:12-17, NLT)

Are you wondering how you are going to pay your bills?

Jesus told Peter to go fishing, which was his life trade, and to open the mouth of the first fish he caught. In the fish's mouth, Peter found two coins, enough to pay both Jesus' and his own taxes. Jesus can bring supernatural provision for you too when you are wondering, "How am I ever going to pay these bills?" Jesus may not send you fishing, but His ways are limitless, surpassing human ingenuity and ability. When you ask God for financial or other provision, be sure not to "box" Him in by your own limited understanding!

Be open to unusual, creative strategies, and downright miracles, that God will use to take care of your need. When you hear His voice, which will always agree with His Word, follow whatever direction He gives you, and watch Him work lovingly in your behalf. Praise the Lord for His goodness and mercy, and expect good things, not bad things to happen. God will come through for you if you trust and do not doubt!

An interesting thing happened to me one evening—a supernatural touch by the hand of God. I was driving to church, getting a little concerned about being late as I was scheduled to serve in one of the ministries that evening.

It was dark outside and in my car, some of the dashboard lights—not the odometer—but the clock light and others, hadn't worked in two years. I had gotten used to not knowing what time it was when I was driving at night, but this time, I was thinking, "I sure wish I could tell what time it is!" Glancing down at the dashboard clock not expecting to see anything, all of a sudden it was brightly lit and I could see the time clearly: 6:42 pm. This may seem like a little thing, but it's one example of how God will make a supernatural way to bring the provision when we have a need. There were no natural means by which that clock should have been lit, but God is good! He wanted me to have peace to know that I was going to get where I was going on time!

You can heal the sick and set the captives free, in Jesus' Name!

Jesus empowered His disciples to go out in His Name and heal the sick during His life on earth, after His life on earth, and still today! In fact, Jesus said His disciples would do even more miracles than He did, because Jesus' physical lifespan upon the earth was short. Jesus ascended to heaven, to be at the right hand of the Father, interceding for you, your loved ones, and your needs. He is cheering you on as you, along with millions of other believers, carry out the work He began, teaching the Good News and setting the captives free!

> *"I tell you the truth, anyone who believes in me will do the same works I have done, and even greater works, because I am going to be*

177

with the Father. You can ask for anything in
my name (according to God's will and ways),
and I will do it, so that the Son can bring
glory to the Father. Yes, ask me for anything in
my name, and I will do it!

(John 14:12-14, NLT)

Peter and John were one example of Jesus' followers healing the sick in the authority of Jesus' Name. Through their faith and acting on what Jesus had promised, a crippled man was made whole!

1 One day Peter and John were going up to
the temple at the time of prayer—at three in
the afternoon.

2 Now a man crippled from birth was being
carried to the temple gate called Beautiful,
where he was put every day to beg from those
going into the temple courts.

3 When he saw Peter and John about to enter,
he asked them for money.

4 Peter looked straight at him, as did John.
Then Peter said, "Look at us!"

5 So the man gave them his attention,
expecting to get something from them.

6 Then Peter said, "Silver or gold I do not
have, but what I have I give you. In the name
of Jesus Christ of Nazareth, walk."

7 Taking him by the right hand, he helped him
up, and instantly the man's feet and ankles
became strong.

*8 He jumped to his feet and began to walk.
Then he went with them into the temple courts,
walking and jumping, and praising God.*

*9 When all the people saw him walking and
praising God,*

*10 they recognized him as the same man who
used to sit begging at the temple gate called
Beautiful, and they were filled with wonder
and amazement at what had happened to him.*

(Acts 3:1-10, NIV)

Watch your words...

o   Your words must line up with the Word of God!
o   Faith and power words activate healing and other miracles!
o   Refuse to allow yourself to believe and speak the worst!

What you say is vital to receiving your healing...your miracle provision...or anything else in the supernatural kingdom life. The Bible says that "out of the abundance of the heart, the mouth speaks." What you believe in your heart will eventually come out in your speaking. Numerous Scriptures show the importance of keeping your words (and your heart) lined up with the Word and ways of God.

*The tongue can bring death or life; those who
love to talk will reap the consequences.*

(Proverbs 18:21, NLT)

22 And Jesus, replying, said to them, Have faith in God [constantly].

23 Truly I tell you, whoever says to this mountain, Be lifted up and thrown into the sea! and does not doubt at all in his heart but believes that what he says will take place, it will be done for him.

24 For this reason I am telling you, whatever you ask for in prayer, believe (trust and be confident) that it is granted to you, and you will [get it].

25 And whenever you stand praying, if you have anything against anyone, forgive him and let it drop (leave it, let it go), in order that your Father Who is in heaven may also forgive you your [own] failings and shortcomings and let them drop.

(Mark 11:22-25, AMP)

Notice the emphasis in this Scripture portion, commonly quoted as an example of faith without wavering, of the words we speak. The right words will come out of a heart filled with unshakeable faith! Faith in a heart is not active and productive until it is spoken and acted upon.

May I also take just a moment here to point out the last verse, which shows the tremendous importance of making sure our hearts are right before God, particularly in the area of forgiveness. If we are holding something against someone, especially husbands and wives (see 1 Peter 3:8), but really it applies to everyone; our prayers will be hindered. The answers to prayer that we are seeking, except for God's mercy, will not come until we make things right with God and with others.

Focus Your Mind and Heart...
o Be transformed by renewing your mind to the Word of God.
o Out of your heart come the issues of life.
o Keep your mind and heart focused on Jesus.

Do you want to have perfect peace that passes human understanding, undisturbed composure, no matter what is happening around you? The Scriptures say you can if you keep your mind fixed on Jesus, knowing that God loves you and will take care of you. In order to receive miracles that go beyond human logic and ability, you will have to learn to believe that with God, all things are possible to him who believes.

> *Be anxious for nothing, but in everything by*
> *prayer and supplication, with thanksgiving,*
> *let your requests be made known to God;*
> *and the peace of God, which surpasses all*
> *understanding, will guard your hearts and*
> *minds through Christ Jesus.*
>
> (Philippians 4:6-7, NKJV)

> *For with God nothing is ever impossible and*
> *no word from God shall be without power or*
> *impossible of fulfillment.*
>
> (Luke 1:37, AMP)

Through God's miracle-working power, you can overcome danger, and rise above natural circumstances. If you are walking in the kingdom life God has planned for you, you can even eat or drink poison and it will not hurt you. This famous Scripture in Mark says the believer can cast out demons and lay hands on the sick and the sick will recover. Praise the Lord!

> *And these signs will follow those who believe:*
> *In My name they will cast out demons; they*
> *will speak with new tongues; they will take up*
> *serpents; and if they drink anything deadly,*
> *it will by no means hurt them; they will lay*
> *hands on the sick, and (the sick) will recover...*
> *And they went out and preached everywhere,*
> *the Lord working with them and confirming*
> *the word through the accompanying signs.*
>
> (Mark 16:17-18, 20, NKJV)

Abiding in God brings divine protection...

o   God promises divine protection and safety when you abide in Him.

o   It isn't automatic just because we are believers; we must stay in Him.

o   Your faith, your words, and your mind must agree with what God says.

Friend, God does not intend for you to walk in fear if you know His Son, Jesus. As you draw close to Him and live under His covering, you can have the all-encompassing promise of God's divine protection operating in your life no matter how devastating and dismal your circumstances may seem. (See Psalm 91 below.)

1 Those who live in the shelter of the Most High will find rest in the shadow of the Almighty.

2 This I declare about the LORD: He alone is my refuge, my place of safety; he is my God, and I trust him.

3 For he will rescue you from every trap and protect you from deadly disease.

4 He will cover you with his feathers. He will shelter you with his wings. His faithful promises are your armor and protection.

5 Do not be afraid of the terrors of the night, nor the arrow that flies in the day.

6 Do not dread the disease that stalks in darkness, nor the disaster that strikes at midday.

7 Though a thousand fall at your side, though ten thousand are dying around you, these evils will not touch you.

8 Just open your eyes, and see how the wicked are punished.

9 If you make the LORD your refuge, if you make the Most High your shelter,

10 no evil will conquer you; no plague will come near your home.

11 For he will order his angels to protect you wherever you go.

12 They will hold you up with their hands so you won't even hurt your foot on a stone.

13 You will trample upon lions and cobras; you will crush fierce lions and serpents under your feet!

14 The LORD says, "I will rescue those who love me. I will protect those who trust in my name.

15 When they call on me, I will answer; I will be with them in trouble. I will rescue and honor them.

16 I will reward them with a long life and give them my salvation."

(Psalm 91, NLT)

Wow! What a phenomenal promise of divine protection. Some things that could potentially harm us, God never allows to get near us or cross our path. At other times, He may deliver us out of the danger or attack. If you follow the conditions of this psalm, God promises to keep you, your family, your house and your possessions safe, free from sickness and loss. Sound too good to be true? It's not! Change your thinking—ALL things are possible with God!

But, once again, I need to remind you, this promise is for believers who walk daily in their covenant relationship with Jesus, whose minds and hearts are fixed upon Him, who obey the voice of the Holy Spirit (the Spirit of God) within them when He tells them, "Do this," or "Don't do that…don't go there," etc. God speaks to us in a still, small voice. When we listen and obey, then we are protected, and can receive whatever we need (that agrees with His Word and will).

God promises help to those who seek Him…
o   Communicate with God daily in prayer as you would talk with your best friend.
o   Spend time thanking and praising God; cultivate an awareness of God's presence.
o   Study, believe, and act on what you see in the Word of God (the Bible).

There may come a day when it isn't popular to read the Bible; even to the place where authorities may pass a law and forcefully take away the Bible from American life. The Scriptures teach that the Word of God is like a lamp unto our path, shining and guiding us in the good and right way to go, and that it is wise to "hide" the Word in our hearts so that we might not sin. Knowing, believing, and acting upon the Scriptures keep us going in the right direction; they keep us healed, protected, walking in God's provision, and operating in God's wisdom.

Consequently, faith comes from hearing the message, and the message is heard through the word of Christ.

(Romans 10:17, NIV)

Hide God's Word in your heart today and every day!

Take time to not only study, but to memorize a life-giving, faith-producing Scripture from the Bible every day. Soon, you will have much of the Bible "hidden" in your heart. Keep repeating these Scriptures each day, so they stay fresh, meaningful, and alive in your heart! This practice will build your faith to a higher place, and it will keep you from being deceived in the end times that we are living in. People, who operate under the devil's direction and power, may try to steal what you have in Christ. They may take your physical possessions, even your life, but they can never take from you what is firmly planted in your heart. Hide God's Word in heart today and every day!

With my whole heart have I sought You, inquiring for and of You and yearning for You; Oh, let me not wander or step aside [either in ignorance or willfully] from Your commandments. Your word have I laid up in my heart, that I might not sin against You.

(Psalm 119:10-11, AMP)

It may seem like an overwhelming task to accomplish all these things. And, it would be if we had to do them in our strength and with our limited human abilities. But, the good news is that the more we walk with Jesus, the easier it gets to walk the way He walked…to do the things He did…to live above the limitations of the world.

Miracles prove Jesus is who He says He is

To the "religious" world…

(A religious ruler) came to Jesus by night and said to Him, "Rabbi, we know that You are a teacher come from God for no one can do these signs that You do unless God is with him."

(John 3:2, NKJV)

To the "unbelieving" world…

"But I have a greater witness than John's; for the works which the Father has given Me to finish—the very works that I do—bear witness of Me that the Father has sent Me."

(John 3:2, NKJV)

Many churches and ministries give out food and "medicine," but I believe we are living in a day where God wants us to give out food and "MIRACLES." The Church has been called to be a place where the gifts of the Holy Spirit are in operation…where believers lay hands on the sick and the sick recover.

God has given me an evangelistic and healing ministry, called Jesus Healing House, which combines teaching about Jesus, prayer, and ministering in the gifts of the Spirit in a community setting for ALL people...believers and unbelievers alike. This ministry outreach is a model of what I believe the Lord is calling us to do in, and through, every church that believes God does miracles today.

Jesus Healing House also offers a training program that provides opportunities for the body of Christ to be equipped to use their God-given spiritual and ministry gifts. (See Mark 16:15-18, Ephesians 4:12, 16, and 1 Corinthians 12.)

If you would like more information or assistance in establishing a Jesus Healing House through your church or group of churches, please feel free to contact me as follows:

> Holly Lewerenz
> Jesus Healing House Ministries
> P.O. Box 31883
> Chicago, IL 60631
> Phone: (817) 285-0058
> Email: Holly@HealingforAmerica.com

You will find more information on Jesus Healing House (God's Glory Care Centers) in the next chapter *Especially for Pastors: A Message and Model.*

**It is your choice whether to live in
the world's system which is failing,
or in God's glorious kingdom system
which never fails.**

Any country, city, workplace, school, home or other group has ground rules. There are certain things you have to do to live successfully within the framework of the group. The kingdom of God is no different. Salvation is a free gift of God's grace, but to live victoriously in God's kingdom system, you will have to follow the "rules." Actually, these are not so much "dos" and "don'ts," as they are principles that will work for you if you believe, and put them into practice in your daily life!

Do not get discouraged though when you think of having to follow a list of "To Do's." The world can be a hard taskmaster, but Jesus' way is not hard. In fact, His way will actually relieve your weariness and heavy burdens.

> *Then Jesus said, "Come to me, all of you who are weary and carry heavy burdens, and I will give you rest. Take my yoke upon you. Let me teach you, because I am humble and gentle at heart, and you will find rest for your souls. For my yoke is easy to bear, and the burden I give you is light."*
>
> (Matthew 11:28-30, NLT)

Some of the basics of living in God's kingdom system include:

o The God kind of faith
o Repentance when you've missed it
o Walking in love toward God and others
o Patience: Sometimes "instant" miracles occur—and oh, how we love those times! But occasionally, we will have to exercise our patience from the time we ask for the answer, miracle or provision, until its manifestation.
o Timing: immediate obedience works best! As soon as we hear the voice of God and know that it is Him, we

189

should pray for clarification and understanding; then, be quick to act in accordance to His direction.

o Praise: God inhabits our praises, and where God's presence is, that is where the miracles will be found! Apart from the presence and power of God, there cannot be supernatural provision.

o A childlike trust: A child believes his father can do ANYTHING. You tell a little boy or girl that their father can't do something, and they won't believe you. A father is BIG in the trusting eyes of his son or daughter… "My father can beat your father, my father is faster than your father, or my father can do this or that better than anybody," Dad's little boy or girl may boast.

o Reliance upon the Spirit of God and His ways, which don't always line up with human wisdom and philosophy.

1 And I, brethren, when I came to you, did not come with excellence of speech or of wisdom declaring to you the testimony of God.

2 For I determined not to know anything among you except Jesus Christ and Him crucified.

3 I was with you in weakness, in fear, and in much trembling.

4 And my speech and my preaching were not with persuasive words of human wisdom, but in demonstration of the Spirit and of power,

5 that your faith should not be in the wisdom of men but in the power of God.

(1 Corinthians 2:1-5, NKJV)

As mentioned in chapter four *The Church's Finest Hour: Joseph's Storehouse and Other Remedies,* there may come a time when hospitals, healthcare, the government welfare system, and many other things we take for granted are no longer available. There may be food shortages or famine, and what food we get, may not contain all the best nutrients.

Then, we will have to believe in miracles and live in the realm of supernatural provision!

You might as well make up your mind and your will to learn to live in God's kingdom system and by His supernatural provision and methods NOW, so you'll be prepared for the time when you have no choice.

In times past, when sickness, disease or injury has attacked my body or mind, I have followed these steps:

o Recognize that sickness or attack is never from God! He is a good God. Sickness comes from the devil or from our own foolish actions.

o Seek out in the Bible, Scriptures that pertain to my situation; speak them out in faith, believing that God will bring them to pass in my situation.

o Pray, asking God to heal me according to the Scriptures I just mentioned; also in the authority of Jesus' Name, and in the power of His blood and His Spirit.

o Praise God and thank Him for the healing (or other answer) that is already on the way.

There are many Word-based DVDs, CDs and books available that will help build your faith to receive God's healing and provision. Take advantage of these resources in addition to—but not in place of—the Bible. Such materials will encourage you, and when they contain the Word of God, there is a real anointing power from God's Spirit in them that will literally bring healing to your body and mind.

I have many great tapes and books, but I will share with you my favorite. It is called *God's Healing Word,* a collection of healing Scriptures, which is ministered by Creflo A. Dollar, worldwide Bible teacher and pastor, and is available on a CD. You can order *God's Healing Word* by visiting Dr. Dollar's website at www.creflodollarministries. org. God has used this tape and others multiple times to bring forth my healing. Praise the Name of Jesus!

Chapter Seven

Especially for Pastors:
A Message and Model

This chapter is mainly directed at pastors and other church leadership. If you are not a pastor, but are interested in the following material, please consider showing it to your pastor or other church leadership.

> *Jesus traveled throughout Galilee <u>teaching</u> in the synagogues, <u>preaching</u> everywhere the Good News about the Kingdom. And he <u>healed</u> people who had every kind of sickness and disease. (Underlines added for emphasis and clarity.)*
>
> (Matthew 4:23, NLT)

In the Gospels, we see that Jesus' ministry was three-fold. He not only preached and taught, but also healed the people through the power given Him by His Father. God's Word says Jesus is the same yesterday, today and forever. It is on this premise that Jesus Healing House has been birthed and is carrying out its God-given, Holy Spirit-empowered, Christ-centered mission.

As a leader in Christian ministry, you know the importance of getting the Gospel out to people by every means available.

Sickness, bondage, depression, and hopelessness abounds everywhere... In spite of our fitness-centered lifestyle, people battle sickness in their bodies, mental anguish in their minds, and emotional hurts in their hearts. Never in the history of the world has there been so much pain and suffering! Along with the normal challenges of everyday life added to the current economic and political crises, it is evident that stress levels are soaring.

With the threat of nuclear strike at our coasts and internally, economic upheaval is mounting daily. With our faith in God, in spite of the imminent dangers, we believe that America will stand! I believe this is the hour where the Church must take her place as a "trumpet blower" and instrument of God's saving grace and power.

**What an awesome time and opportunity
to share Jesus with a hurting world!**

God promises good to His people! He is not far away from them. He is not a distant or disinterested God concerning the daily matters of life. God has a specific plan for His people—individually and corporately—that can only be discerned when we seek Him, entering into and remaining in His presence.

*For I know the plans I have for you," declares
the LORD, "plans to prosper you and not to
harm you, plans to give you hope and a future.
Then you will call upon me and come and
pray to me, and I will listen to you. You will
seek me and find me when you seek me with
all your heart.*

(Jeremiah 29:11-13, NIV)

Pastor, your church can be God's instrument of evangelism in a greater way than ever before as a "servant" of the community in these critical times. Jesus said that he who would be the greatest should be the servant of all. Serving your community, in a time of famine, by administering the love of Jesus to them through the practical means of food distribution as well as the "spiritual food" of the Gospel will be a much-needed ministry! You can be a leader in uniting local churches in your community and organizing a harmony of efforts between churches to fulfill Christ's mandate of love in response to the fears and challenges of the coming days. This will open up a widespread opportunity for people to turn to the Lord and become born-again.

You can be a "Joseph"—proclaiming the spiritual meaning behind world events just as God through Joseph revealed the meaning of Pharaoh's dreams. You can play a strategic role in sounding the alarm that it is time to awake—and repent—for the coming of the Lord is near! Joseph not only accurately interpreted the meaning of Pharaoh's dreams, but he came up with the plan to save

Egypt—a food storehouse and distribution plan, which is the inspiration behind what I call "Joseph's Storehouse" (more details later in this chapter.)

In those days, Joseph was sent by God, but he worked through the "government" to carry out His plan. Today, I believe that in the plan God showed me, Joseph's counterpart is the Church. We have a much greater covenant with our Lord Jesus than Joseph had under the old covenant. Not only can the Church provide physical food, we can provide spiritual, life-sustaining benefits. Jesus is the Way not only to wholeness in spiritual salvation, but in physical, emotional and mental healing, deliverance from fear and addictions, and much more!

The role of the church

Jesus commissioned believers to preach the Gospel and to heal the sick. The leaders of the Church are called to teach and equip the saints to do the work of ministry. You will see on the next page a chart showing what I call God's Glory Care Centers. These include a four-part outreach that will minister to the needs of both your church and community today:

(1) The Prayer Center

(2) Joseph's Storehouse

(3) The Believers Ministry Training Center

(4) Jesus Healing House

VISION FOR YOUR CHURCH & COMMUNITY
GOD'S GLORY
Care Centers

What? A church center as described below established in these end times to meet the desperate needs of people—spiritual, mental, emotional, and physical healing, and basic necessities such as food for families—during a time of worldwide crisis.

Where? Churches and community site locations which are organized and directed under the legal and spiritual covering of local church leadership and are staffed with trained and qualified church volunteers.

Why? To reach the world with the Gospel of Jesus Christ, the message of God's love and healing power; to grow believers into spiritual maturity and equip them for ministry; and to see the fullness of God's GLORY upon the earth!

(1) PRAYER CENTER
Foundation for ministry must be centered on prayer and God's Word. A place where believers can meet together or visit individually to intercede for their community, America, Israel, and the world. This will be a major support for the three other outreach components.

(2) JOSEPH'S STOREHOUSE
♥ Distribution of food and other needs ♥ This will most likely be the entry place for people who have been devastated by the worldwide economic crisis, a place where the church can show the compassionate reality of Christ and lead these people into the safe haven of God's kingdom. From here, they can visit the healing center for ministry, or enter into regular church life to grow spiritually and fulfill God's plan for their destiny.

(3) TRAINING CENTER
Offers a believers' ministry training program to provide opportunities for the body of Christ to be equipped to use their God-given spiritual and ministry gifts. Believers are taught through the Word as well as through impartation of the Holy Spirit to minister to those who will come to the God's Glory Care Center.

(4) HEALING CENTER
Implements a three-fold concept including:
1) Showing of the world-acclaimed JESUS movie, or abbreviated version.
2) Teaching on healing and related biblical principles from God's Word.
3) Prayer and ministry by anointed and trained ministry workers.

197

How will my church benefit?

Pastor, you have many decisions to make regarding which ministry outreaches and programs will best fit the mission God has given your church. You want to reach your community and win the lost to Christ; yet you need to provide teaching and opportunities for your congregation to mature in the Lord and be equipped for service. These days, the Lord is calling His church and His people back to basics. Time is short until Jesus returns; so we need to get serious about "going" and bringing in the harvest. The God's Glory Care Center outreach is powerful in its simplicity because its total focus is on sharing the Good News of Jesus Christ!

God's Glory Care Centers, which encompass Jesus Healing House and Joseph's Storehouse, is an extended arm of the Church—breaking barriers and crossing over denominational lines. GGCC seeks to help the Church by organizing an effective evangelistic outreach to their communities. GGCC also offers a believers ministry training program that provides opportunities for the body of Christ to be equipped to use their God-given spiritual and ministry gifts. (See Mark 16:15-18, Ephesians 4:12, 16; and 1 Corinthians 12.) God's Glory Care Centers, under the legal name of Jesus Healing House Ministries, is a Texas-chartered, 501(c)(3) non-profit organization. For further information, please contact Holly Lewerenz at (817) 285-0058.

As you reach out to your community, know that God will bless you abundantly because there is nothing more important to Him than reaching the lost and healing the hurts of our generation in the Name and power of our Lord Jesus Christ. Beside the rich, warm satisfaction of fulfilling your end-time call and seeing many saved, healed and restored, your church will be increased in numbers and with the simplicity and vitality of new life infused by an influx of new "little lambs" that the Lord will entrust to your care.

Depending on the selected location, and whether the facilities are rented, donated, or owned, as well as other factors, would determine the frequency of your God's Glory Care Center ministry; i.e., one day a week, or every day. Jesus taught and healed on the Sabbath. I believe Saturdays would be a good choice to begin GGCC, though this could develop into a daily operation. Prayerfully seek the Lord's direction as to which components of God's Glory Care Centers He would call you to implement at your church. It may be one or all four centers depending on His mission for your church, the need in the community, your budget and willingness to enter into this end-time effort to reach the lost for Christ.

This can be, of course, but does not have to be a large operation. My first center which combines elements 1, 3 and 4 on the chart is only a small 780-square-foot, rented, retail storefront located in Dallas, Texas. This outreach is organized and operated by an independent Christian ministry rather than a church. See the next page for a sample window sign that would give people an understanding of your services:

Everybody Welcome!

Who We Are...

Jesus Healing House Ministries
(Shady Oaks Shopping Center)
423 W. Bedford Euless Road • Hurst, TX 76053

For more information, please call: (817) 285-0058

What We Offer...

Prayer:
For healing (physical, emotional, spiritual, addictions)
Other needs (financial, relationships, job, and more)

Healing: Private or Group Sessions Available.

Bible Principles for Your Healing

Bombarded by all the latest information on how to get healed and stay healthy? This class is different. It's not a nutrition or exercise class. We don't focus on the do's and don'ts. We teach you how to receive God's healing through sound biblical principles. Join this class and believe that you will receive God's miracle in your life.

Learn How to Pray for the Sick

If you are a Christian believer, you already know the Bible says you can "lay hands on the sick and they will recover" (Mark 16:18). But how? Have you longed to be used by God but unsure that He would really use you to pray for the sick and others who are hurting? Join this class and begin to walk in all that God has called you to do!

ADDITIONAL CLASSES:
(CALL FOR CLASS DATES & DESCRIPTIONS.)

Counseling: Individuals or groups.

Saturday:	**11:00 am—4:00 pm**
Monday - Tuesday:	**7:00—9:00 pm**
Thursday - Friday:	**7:00—9:00 pm**

There is no charge for our services. Jesus Healing House Ministries is a non-profit Christian organization. All services are provided according to a faith-based, biblical perspective. Licensed Christian minister is available.

The following information offers a model for establishing a God's Glory Care Center in your church or community. The guidelines are brief and generalized enough to allow plenty of room for creativity and adaptation to the specific church, leadership preferences, community needs and other resources already available. Though, I caution you, do not think, "Well, somebody else, or some other church, or the government agency is already doing this work." Darkness is increasing…the economy and other end-time conditions are not going to get better; they are going to get worse! Every Christian and every church must fulfill their God-called and God-empowered part!

The Prayer Center
(Center #1 on the chart on page 197)

In Isaiah 56:7, God says, *"…For My house shall be called a house of prayer for all nations."* And, Jesus, again referred to His Father's house as being a house of prayer—after He chased the merchants and money changers out of the Temple. Several additional references were made that Jesus frequently spent time with His Father in prayer, sometimes all night.

In the Prayer Center, a number of activities can take place, including:

(1) Ongoing prayer groups and individual prayer during the open hours of the prayer center for your community, America, Israel and the nations as well as for people's personal needs.

(2) Foundational prayer for your church, its services, staff, needs and ministries.

(3) To house a telephone call-in prayer ministry or walk-in ministry for anyone who has a need for prayer.

(4) This could also be a place where salvation teaching and prayer for those people who will come to Joseph's Storehouse could be a part of the procedure for their receiving food and other basic necessities. Many current day missions and Christian food pantries require this procedure in order to be sure that people are getting the "spiritual food" of the Gospel as well as physical food.

(5) A place of worship, praise unto the Lord, seeking His presence and ministering unto Him (Acts 13: 1-2).

(6) Regular times of intercession for the Healing Center (Jesus Healing House), for the needs of those who will receive ministry, and for those who will minister. They will need to stay "prayed up" and in the presence of God to walk in the anointing of the Holy Spirit to do the works that Jesus did (John 14:12). Prayer and God's Word must be the foundation of Jesus Healing House.

(7) Classes and ministry training for prayer ministers and others who want to increase their knowledge and skill in effective prayer intercession.

Joseph's Storehouse
(Center #2 on the chart on page 197)

In chapter four *The Church's Finest Hour: Joseph's Storehouse and Other Remedies* you first read about the vision God gave me that we, in the Church of today, are to recreate the plan God gave Joseph in the Old Testament to save Egypt and the neighboring lands during a seven-year period of famine. As explained in that chapter, I do see some major differences. First of all, I believe this is to be a ministry of the Church, not a hook-up to government programs, which I believe may fail because of the financial crisis, or may not be available to any person or group who does not receive the mark of the antichrist that would allow them to buy or sell.

We are going to have to depend on two things:

(1) The generosity and love of God shown through believers, as they are directed and enabled by God to give.

(2) The supernatural provision of God that will supercede the economic limitations and natural sources of supply.

Also as mentioned previously, I do not want to place anyone under the law and say they must "tithe" or give a specified portion of either their income or a donation of canned food and other imperishable goods. This is solely up to each individual to do as God instructs and provides. In the story of Joseph, the percentage of the crop that was set aside and stored to be available for the years of famine was 20%, or one-fifth. Everyone can share a little or a lot, according to their heart and financial ability. This reminds me of the story of Elisha and the widow, during a time of drought in the land:

8 Then the Lord said to Elijah,

9 "Go and live in the village of Zarephath, near the city of Sidon. I have instructed a widow there to feed you."

10 So he went to Zarephath. As he arrived at the gates of the village, he saw a widow gathering sticks, and he asked her, "Would you please bring me a little water in a cup?"

11 As she was going to get it, he called to her, "Bring me a bite of bread, too."

12 But she said, "I swear by the Lord your God that I don't have a single piece of bread in the house. And I have only a handful of flour left in the jar and a little cooking oil in the bottom of the jug. I was just gathering a few sticks to cook this last meal, and then my son and I will die."

13 But Elijah said to her, "Don't be afraid! Go ahead and do just what you've said, but make a little bread for me first. Then use what's left to prepare a meal for yourself and your son.

14 For this is what the Lord, the God of Israel, says: There will always be flour and olive oil left in your containers until the time when the Lord sends rain and the crops grow again!"

*15 So she did as Elijah said, and she and
Elijah and her son continued to eat for many
days.*

*16 There was always enough flour and olive
oil left in the containers, just as the Lord had
promised through Elijah.*

(1 Kings 17:8-16, NLT)

People who are helped through the food ministry or those who cannot afford to give to the food ministry can help in other ways. They can volunteer their time, the work of their hands, and prayer.

An interesting note in the Joseph story is that this grain was not given out freely, but sold. When the people's money ran out, they "paid" with their livestock, their homes, and finally their own bodies, becoming slaves to Pharaoh. Often, dependence on government programs leads people into "slavery," having to follow someone's else's rules and restrictions. Before the end of the seven-year famine in Egypt, everyone had become slaves to Pharaoh and none owned their own land or lives. The exception was Joseph and his family who had favor with Pharaoh for a season, and the priests that were in the land. They were not charged for the grain or their possessions required in exchange for food. Freedom truly does come in following God!

Seek God—and wise counsel for
guidelines when you start

As your church is beginning a food ministry, seek God for His guidelines. There are many poor even now in the country that are dependent on welfare and food pantries. However, it would be wise to do some research of food ministries that are currently operating successfully. In the Bible it says that he who does not work does not eat, so it is good to encourage responsibility in those coming for help. Firstly, use this opportunity as a time to lead them to Christ, or to strengthen their walk with Him if they are already Christians. Secondly, there should be some kind of "application" process to ensure that there truly is a significant need in the recipient that cannot be met through working or help from other family members. These would factor in their income, expenses and other considerations. This would help to guard against waste and unnecessary use so that supplies would be available for the "poor and needy," not the " poor and greedy."

In a time of financial crisis, of course, needs will increase and many more than usual will need a helping hand. But, especially in this case, we want to be sure not to indiscriminately use up the food supply. When famine becomes a reality in America, as well as in other nations worldwide, we must use discernment and wisdom to save and store enough for the times that lay ahead, rather than using all of the resources now. Each church will have to decide what God would have them to do in this regard. Perhaps, it would be wise to save at least one-fifth (as in Joseph's story) of the donated food and other basic supplies in a "Joseph's Storehouse" for the future need, or perhaps the other way around; distribute one-fifth now to fill the current need of your congregation and community, and lay aside the remaining four-fifths in a "Joseph's Storehouse" for the future need. Or, it could be half and half…God will lead you.

In the time of famine and need, those who have been blessed by God with provisions should pay for the food if possible rather than receiving it for free; in this way they will continue to receive the blessing that God promises to those who give liberally, and also the church food supplies may be increased and amply available for those who cannot afford to pay.

One pastor I heard of recently who operates a food ministry through his church asked the members of his congregation to bring cans of food because supplies were getting low. He offered that if they brought in 10 canned items, the church would give them a free tape of one of his sermons. Cool idea! The poor got physically fed, and those who gave were spiritually fed!

In Old Testament days, it was common practice in Israel (Leviticus 19:9-10) for the workers in the field as they were harvesting the crops to leave a little for the poor to glean, or to come along after the harvesters, to pick up the "leftovers" for their own families. In this way, the poor received the food they needed, but did have to put in some effort (work) to obtain it. Look at this beautiful example from the book of Ruth:

> *6 So the servant who was in charge of the reapers answered and said, "It is the young Moabite woman who came back with Naomi from the country of Moab.*

7 And she said, 'Please let me glean and gather after the reapers among the sheaves.' So she came and has continued from morning until now, though she rested a little in the house."...

15 And when she rose up to glean, Boaz (the owner of the field) commanded his young men, saying, "Let her glean even among the sheaves, and do not reproach her.

16 Also let grain from the bundles fall purposely for her; leave it that she may glean, and do not rebuke her."

17 So she gleaned in the field until evening, and beat out what she had gleaned, and it was about an ephah of barley...

(Ruth 2: 6-7, 15-17, NKJV)

A food ministry in action…

An excellent example of a fruitful food ministry in action is located in Haltom City, Texas. Riverwalk Fellowship's "Feed the Multitudes" food ministry program under the leadership of senior pastor, Steve Solomon, has been operating successfully since 1994. Hundreds are being fed weekly at Riverwalk, and Pastor Solomon has graciously allowed me to share the following information as a helpful model to other pastors.

You can also find this and other information on their website riverwalkfellowship.com. or at Riverwalk Fellowship, 5612 Glenview Drive, Haltom City, TX 76117. The church phone number is (817) 577-9673.

Riverwalk Fellowship
Feed the Multitudes Food Ministry

Feed the Multitudes Food Ministry is a 501 (c) 3 Non-Profit organization that began fourteen years ago. In that time we have fed and clothed more than two hundred thousand families. We have met the needs of individuals in the surrounding cities in many ways. This ministry has changed the lives of so many people including myself and the many volunteers that have faithfully assisted in this food ministry over the years. The national average for a family is 4.5 people.

I. Preparation for our Weekly Food Distribution
    A. Every Monday volunteers from Riverwalk Fellowship as well as other people that support this ministry meet from 4:00 PM to 8:30 PM to prepare for the following day's distribution.
    B. On Monday morning a volunteer driver picks up the food we have ordered the previous week from a local Food Bank.
        1. Monday evening begins with group prayer.
        2. Volunteers fill sacks to prepare for up to 400 families, as well as inventory what we have.
        3. Our 24' truck is unloaded and food is separated to be filled into the sacks or stored on pallets for the following week.
        4. Volunteers clean and mop the storage area and prepare for next week's distribution by organizing the food.
        5. Filled sacks are then loaded onto our truck and driven back to Riverwalk for Tuesday's distribution.

    C. We store our food in a warehouse that we lease and its rent is donated to us.

    D. Our 24' Diesel Mitsubishi Truck with lift was purchased from donations given by members of Riverwalk as well as other people that support this ministry.

II. Tuesday's Food Distribution

    A. We have approximately 50 volunteers that meet at Riverwalk at 6:30 AM to begin the day's ministry. We feed approximately 400 families per week. That is approximately 1800 people per week, based on the national average of 4.5 people per family. Due to the large and increasing number of clients, we have had to begin to split the services. Clients with last names beginning with A through L come the first and third Tuesdays. Clients with last names beginning with M through Z come the second and fourth Tuesdays of the month. Months that have a fifth Tuesday we do not have a food distribution; we do an outreach where we distribute food to a local area (homes or apartments) where there is need.

      1. Tuesdays begin with group prayer.

      2. Each volunteer is assigned a position.

         a. Unloading sacks from the truck.

         b. Sorting and bagging frozen meat and vegetables picked up from a local vendor that donates on a weekly basis.

         c. Sorting and packing breads and desserts donated from a local bread vendor.

         d. Setting out traffic cones to direct traffic for distribution.

    e. All volunteers wear orange traffic vest for safety and for our clients to easily identify a volunteer for any assistance they may need.

B. The foyer outside our sanctuary is then prepared for the day's needs.

    1. Tables are set up for first time clients that will need to complete an application.

    2. Information from the application is entered later on a database and all applications are filed and maintained.

    3. Computer printouts are set up along with numbers that will be given to each client to pickup their food.

    4. We have both English and Spanish speaking volunteers for our clients.

    5. Many clients will have additional needs such as medical, mortgage payments or monthly rent, clothes and/or diapers. There are other organizations that assist with rent and medical needs and we can refer them to these agencies. We do have clothes and diapers donated occasionally and then can meet those needs also.

C. Doors open at 8:30 AM. Clients are then greeted by our volunteers and directed into our sanctuary for our weekly service.

    1. We have Prayer from 9:00 AM until 9:30 AM.

    2. We have Praise & Worship from 9:30 AM until 10:00 AM

    3. We have a Worship service from 10:00 AM until 10:30 AM.

    4. We have a Spanish interpreter for this service.

D. Clients are dismissed from the sanctuary at 10:30 AM
1. They are then directed to our tables where they pick up their numbers for food pickup or complete an application first and then pick up their number.
2. They then go to their cars and get in line to drive around for their food.
3. A volunteers will put their sack of groceries into their car.
4. Another volunteer will put their bags of frozen meat and vegetables into their car.
5. And another volunteer will put their bread and desserts into their car.
6. Many of our clients will request additional prayers or may just want to talk to one of our volunteers while waiting in their cars. Our volunteers are always ready to pray with or just minister to each individual as may be needed.
7. We strongly believe that our prayers before all activities which take place on Monday and Tuesday; our worship service, and our close relationship with each of our clients are what has caused this food ministry to continue to grow and reach out to the needs of our neighborhood.
E. Clients that come late or cannot stay for our services are requested to come back at 10:30 AM to pick up their groceries and we serve them at that time.

III. Quarterly Outreach
A. Every third month we go out into the neighborhood.

1. We receive a large donation from a national vendor that allows us to distribute food and evangelize at low income apartment complexes.

IV. Holiday Seasons
  A. Thanksgiving
    1. We begin preparing for our Thanksgiving outreach in August.
    2. Vendors are called for donations; we plan to feed 500 families, approximately 2250 people.
    3. By October 1st. we have gathered what has been donated or what has to be purchased, with the exception of the turkeys. Prices for turkeys are not available any earlier than November 1st. We usually purchased five hundred turkeys. All turkeys are usually donated.
    4. A Thanksgiving Holiday meal will consist of a 12 pound turkey, cornbread dressing, green beans, corn, yams, mashed potatoes, cranberry sauce, rolls and a dessert. We present this Holiday basket during our Tuesday distribution service.
  B. The Christmas Holiday is such a special occasion. We again plan to feed 500 families. But, we will also provide at least three very nice wrapped toys for each child.
    1. We start immediately after Thanksgiving getting things ready for Christmas.
    2. We have been collecting toys all year long.
    3. Again we seek as many donations for food as are available.

      4. We then purchase from a local food bank the balance of what is needed.

      5. We provide a complete Holiday meal as we have at Thanksgiving. All hams are usually donated.

      6. Volunteers will wrap all toys for the children. We are usually able to give toys to about 600 children ranging in ages from 6 months to 13 years of age.

      7. Again, we invite the entire family to come on the Tuesday before Christmas to distribute our Christmas baskets of food and toys for the children. We are usually able to give new blankets, coats, hats and gloves to the children.

  C. Number of People Served

      1. In our weekly distribution we serve approximately 1800 people.

      2. In our two big holiday services, we serve approximately 4500 people.

      3. In one year, we serve approximately 93,600 people.

V. Monthly Business Dinner and Annual Appreciation Banquet

  A. Monthly Business Dinner

      1. On the third Tuesday of each month we have an evening meal, discuss how each week has been and any new suggestions from the volunteers of better serving our clients. We also enjoy an evening of fellowship with the volunteers and their families. Each volunteer brings a covered dish for the meal.

B. Annual Appreciation Banquet
   1. This is a time where the church provides all the expenses for a wonderful evening meal.
   2. Each volunteer is recognized for the number of hours they have given to Feed the Multitudes Food Ministry and a Certificate of Appreciation is given. A wonderful time is had by all.

(Thank you to Pastor Steve Solomon, Beverly Johnson and Cheryl Stine for making this information available as a model for other churches to follow in their communities.)

The Believers Ministry Training Center
(Center #3 on the chart on page 197)

The Believer's Ministry Training Program is intended to accommodate staffing and volunteer requirements for the Jesus Healing House ministry outreach. However, it can also serve as a Believers' Equipping Program, which can train believers for service not only in a Jesus Healing House, but also in their church or for personal evangelism in their own daily environment.

An integral part of the Jesus Healing House ministry outreach would be the development of a Believers Ministry Training Program. This can be an ongoing training center at the local church or in combination with a group of local churches to equip believers for the work of ministry at the local Jesus Healing House(s). For more information, or for assistance in setting up either an ongoing believers training program or a one-time series of believers training classes,

please contact me, the author of this book and the founder/
director of God's Glory Care Centers as below:

> Holly Lewerenz
> (God's Glory Care Centers)
> Jesus Healing House Ministries
> P.O. Box 31883
> Chicago, IL 60631
>
> (817) 285-0058
> Holly@HealingforAmerica.com

I would love to hear your thoughts about how this book
has impacted you as well as to assist you in implementing
a God's Glory Care Center in your church and community.

An overview of the Believers
Ministry Training Program

The Believers' Ministry Training Program would
provide opportunities for believers to develop and use
spiritual and ministry gifts. The Bible says that it is the
responsibility of spiritual leaders to equip the body of
Christ for the work of ministry:

> *11 "And He Himself gave some to be apostles,
> some prophets, some evangelists, and some
> pastors and teachers,*
>
> *12 for the equipping of the saints for the work
> of ministry; for the edifying of the body of
> Christ...*
>
> *15 but speaking the truth in love, (they) may
> grow up in all things into Him who is the
> head—Christ—*

*16 from whom the whole body, joined and knit
together by what every (member) supplies,
according to the effective working by which
every part does its share, causes growth of the
body for the edifying of itself in love."*

(Ephesians 4:11, 12, 15, 16, NKJV)

Organizational assistance with curriculum, setting up procedures, training staff and volunteers, and certification can be obtained at Jesus Healing House Ministries (contact information previously given). Other administrative forms and materials such as volunteer standards, statement regarding doctors, medicine, documentation and liability disclaimers, and others, can also be obtained through Jesus Healing House Ministries.

Suggested staff and volunteers include:

- A director to oversee your God's Glory Care Center. This would most likely be a paid staff person as it would probably require a full-time effort.

- Rotating volunteers as needed and available would include:
  - Prayer Coordinator
  - Prayer warriors for ongoing prayer support both on and off operating premises; i.e., intercessors, prayer teams, whomever God calls
  - Prayer ministers to pray and minister God's Word to people individually, sharing biblical truths with them

- Teachers: regular teachers or visiting speakers as called and anointed by God (both to equip JHH workers, and to teach healing classes)

- Registration, greeters, any other support or administrative volunteers as needed

The Believers' Ministry Training Program will provide standard teaching based on the principles in God's Word; however its emphasis is not to be solely on methods and "how to" instruction...a barrage of facts and tons of homework. The focus should be on creating an environment where the Holy Spirit is welcome. Though there should be a well-designed curriculum, we need always to leave room for the Holy Spirit to preempt our plan and guide us in His direction. Class teachers should demonstrate and lead the students in learning by doing—by performing the ministry skill. As they assimilate information, students must learn to rely on hearing the Holy Spirit, following His direction, and yielding to His empowerment and gifts. This can be accomplished as a class, or by dividing up into small groups.

Another way of "learning by doing" is through establishing ministry teams which could be utilized in various ways depending on the nature of the class. For example, the teams could meet in a designated area to witness for the Lord as the students are taking the "Sharing the Gospel of Christ" class. Or, the students can divide up and minister as teams to each other as they are taking the "Praying for the Sick" and "Deliverance Ministry" classes.

There should be some sort of certification or recognition for those who successfully complete the training. Attendance should be mandatory for those who will minister at the local Jesus Healing House. However, completion of the training would not necessarily guarantee acceptance as a JHH prayer minister because only God calls and places people into ministry. One or more of the leaders/teachers who have observed the class participation and lives of the students should be designated to discern those whom God is calling into the Jesus Healing House ministry. Those planning to minister at JHH should also take the healing classes listed in this Jesus Healing House section.

The emphasis of the Believers' Ministry Training Program should not be on grades, but instead on learning and growth in ministry and in the Spirit. Teachers should take into consideration the fact that students have many other responsibilities in life, and plan their schedules accordingly. Much work can be accomplished within the time frame of the class itself with only a reasonable amount of time required outside the class for homework or field experience. However, assignments that are given by the instructor should be completed in order to graduate as well as adequate and active participation by the students during the interactive portions of the class.

Since this would not be an accredited training center (unless the organizing body decided they wanted to obtain accreditation), students would not receive credits that would be transferable to other educational institutions.

However, students deserve and need recognition for their efforts and accomplishments. Acknowledgement of the completion of this program could be in the form of a "Certificate of Completion" issued by the God's Glory Care Center leadership at the church. During the period the class is in session, there could be specific awards given to students for special achievement, i.e., "Successful Ministry to . . ." or "Special Award for Witnessing," or any number of things that could be recognized to build the courage and confidence of the student as well as serve to motivate others. Of course, each student's best reward is the feeling of joy he or she will experience when they see the life-changing effects of their ministry to others and are rewarded for their faithfulness by the Master Himself.

Other important areas to be included in the Believers' Ministry Training Program schedule are as follows:

- Worship, seeking God's presence and glory, prayer and waiting on God

- Developing the student's personal relationship with Christ to receive His anointing

- Encouragement to increase the student's knowledge of God's Word as the foundation of ministry as well as for their personal walk with the Lord

- Interactive ministry: Leaders ministering by example to members of the class, and students learning through ministering to each other in small groups

- Impartation through the laying on of hands of spiritual gifts

"Do not neglect the gift that is in you, which was given to you by prophecy with the laying on of hands of the eldership.

(I Timothy 4:14, NKJV)

Oversight for the local God's Glory Care Center would be the responsibility of the local church or group of churches. Jesus Healing House Ministries could help birth the vision and assist the church in getting started. JHHM can provide guidance, spiritual and ministry resources in the following ways:

- Hold a seminar at your church to include:

  ➢ Impartation of vision and an experience of God's power and glory

  ➢ Believers' Ministry Training Program

  ➢ Training for church representatives to operate JHH ministry program

Many churches already have a wealth of faith-filled, Word-based leaders, teachers, and congregation members that would provide a solid core of ministry workers for the Jesus Healing House. Some of these may be able to be utilized as teachers and facilitators in the Believers Ministry Training Center.

Jesus Healing House

(Center #4 on the chart on page 197)

The purpose of Jesus Healing House is to introduce people to Jesus Christ as their Savior and Lord. In the book of Acts, souls were saved through the preaching of the Word and through miracles by the Holy Spirit leading people to faith in Jesus Christ. Very often, it seemed that signs and wonders (healings, deliverance, etc.) either substantiated the power of God, proving the Word that was preached, or the miracles caused a desire in the hearts of the people to know the God Who performed them. (See Acts 2, 4, 6, 8, 9, 10, 14, as well as others.)

God is truly pouring out His Spirit and doing a great work today, part of which I think, is the development of "believers' ministry." Where it used to be that only great men and women of God—well-known healing evangelists or ministers—would "lay hands on the sick and see them recover;" it seems now that God is indeed pouring out His Spirit on all flesh, and that miracles are manifesting everywhere! The Christian who believes the Word, individually or as part of a ministry team, can lay hands on the sick and see them recover, too. (Mark 16:15-18) Praise God! Even new believers, filled with faith and the power of God's Spirit, can take part in this end-time harvest of souls. It's time! Jesus said,

> 7 *"And as you go, preach, saying, 'the kingdom of heaven is at hand.'*
>
> 8 *Heal the sick, cleanse the lepers, raise the dead, cast out demons"* ...

20 They went out and preached everywhere, the Lord working with them and confirming the Word through the accompanying signs.

(Matthew 10:7-8; Mark 16:20, NKJV)

The ministry outreach of Jesus Healing House is based on the following Bible-based principles:

- **<u>Bringing glory to God through signs and wonders.</u>**
  "So the multitudes marveled when they saw the mute speaking, the maimed made whole, the lame walking and the blind seeing, and they glorified the God of Israel."

  (Matthew 15:31, NKJV)

  "(Nicodemus) said to (Jesus)...no one can do these signs that You do unless God is with Him."

  (John 3:2, NKJV)

- **<u>Sharing the Gospel of Christ to win souls for the kingdom of God.</u>**
  (Immediately following Nicodemus' statement above, Jesus used that opportunity to link His miracles to Nicodemus' need for salvation.)

  "Jesus answered and said to him, 'Most assuredly, I say to you, 'unless one is born again, he cannot see the kingdom of God.'"

  (John 3:3, NKJV)

"For I am not ashamed of the gospel of Christ, for it is the power of God to salvation for everyone who believes."

(Romans 1:16, NKJV)

"... but we preach Christ crucified...Christ the power of God and the wisdom of God."

(I Corinthians 1:23, NKJV)

- **<u>Doing the "works of Jesus" to minister healing and deliverance to people.</u>**
  "Surely He has borne our griefs And carried our sorrows;...But He was wounded for our transgressions, He was bruised for our iniquities; The chastisement for our peace was upon Him, And by His stripes we are healed."

  (Isaiah 53:4-5 NKJV)

  "Bless the Lord, O my soul; And all that is within me, bless His holy name! Bless the Lord, O my soul, And forget not all His benefits: Who forgives all your iniquities, Who heals all your diseases..."

  (Psalm 103:1-3, NKJV)

It is God's will to heal! We have a loving Father who sent His Son, not only to die on the cross to redeem us from sin, but also to purchase our peace, healing, and deliverance. Jesus showed great compassion toward the lost and the hurting during His ministry on earth. And, He has commanded us to follow Him by carrying out His ministry to preach, teach, and heal the sick. With Jesus as our example, and the Holy Spirit as our guide and the power of God, Jesus Healing House can be a mighty work of God to bring in a harvest of souls in these end times. But, it doesn't stop there: Jesus Healing House also ministers to the hurting, sick, and oppressed—both believers and unbelievers—with the power and compassion of our Lord Jesus Christ.

Without a doubt, salvation is the most important need and focus of Christ's commission to His body. However, there are many hurting people—both saved and unsaved— who desperately need God's healing and deliverance as well as salvation. This ministry ranges from one central operation to planting "Jesus Healing Houses" in major cities of the United States and around the world to accomplish the following objectives:

- Lead people to Jesus Christ, bringing to them salvation, healing, and deliverance—spirit, soul and body.

- Provide outreach to those people who might not attend church, or to churchgoers who have not yet experienced the fullness of the Holy Spirit and victorious life in Christ Jesus.

- Provide in-depth teaching to people on how to maintain their healing and walk in abundant health continuously according to God's Word.

A Jesus Healing House could be set up in your church facility, a storefront, community center or other rental location. If located in a storefront-type or community building, I believe this "step out of the Church and into the streets" would meet people where they are and show God's love and miraculous power in an environment and in a way to which they can relate. Everyone (in the world and many even in the Church) get sick: the rich, the poor, the educated, the illiterate, the businessman, homemaker, and laborer—those who love the Lord, those who are skeptics...But God loves them all, and as the Bible repeats over and over: "And Jesus healed them all."

The Jesus Healing House program format includes three components:

PART ONE: The world-acclaimed "Jesus" movie. Watch the blind see, the deaf hear, the lame walk, and every disease healed!

PART TWO: Teaching on the healing ministry of Jesus, especially His redemptive work on the cross, His resurrection, and related principles from the Word of God.

PART THREE: Prayer and personal ministry to individuals for salvation, healing, and other needs.

JESUS Film:

The *JESUS* film was produced by Campus Crusade for Christ. It is based on the Gospel of Luke, showing many healing and deliverance scenes as well as the crucifixion and resurrection of Christ, and has a built-in salvation message at the end. Large numbers of souls have been saved through the viewing of this film, especially in the nations of the world where it has been made available in their own languages. With all of God's abundant blessings on earth, we can sometimes lose sight of Jesus Himself. It's time to focus on why He came—to seek and save the lost that they might inherit eternal life. This video draws viewers' attention to Jesus Christ—what He said, what He did, most of all how His shed blood on the cross purchased our redemption—and how we can follow Him in these last days.

There is also an abbreviated version of the movie *Matthew*, called *Who Is Jesus?* I really like this presentation of the Gospel as it has a good salvation message and invitation at the end, and the entire DVD is only 30 minutes long. It is much easier to get people to sit long enough to view this movie.

You can find permission guidelines for using the *JESUS* film mentioned above on the Jesus Film Project website at www.jesusfilm.org. For *Who Is Jesus?* you can obtain permission guidelines from the International Bible Society before showing this film publicly in your church or Jesus Healing House.

Teaching on Jesus as Savior / Healer

Jesus Healing House provides instruction specifically related to salvation and healing to individuals, small groups, or larger audiences, depending on the scope of the outreach. Some unbelievers who may not want to attend a regular church service or listen to a sermon will attend teaching in a community-based environment which they think will meet their physical needs. Though an overflow of community education on healthy lifestyles and medical information is available, we know the world's system is limited—*but not our God!* Let's demonstrate what the Bible says about Jesus, the Healer and Great Physician, out there in the world! In addition to "live" teaching, a resource area including tapes, videos, books, etc. could be available for supplemental study, either on a giveaway or purchase basis, or a combination of both. This could include an area wherein people can study God's Word and Ministry product resources, or form small groups in which to share what they've learned.

Topics for this teaching portion of Jesus Healing House ministry could include:

- *Origins of Sickness and God's Will to Heal*
- *"He Sent His Word and Healed Them"*
- *The Healing Ministry of Jesus*
- *Foundation of Healing: Christ' Redemptive Work*
- *An Atmosphere of Worship: "God Inhabits Our Praises"*
- *The Holy Spirit: Baptism and Operation of His Gifts*
- *A Lifestyle of Victory in Christ Jesus*

Curriculum is available from Jesus Healing House Ministries.

<u>CAUTIONS</u>

<u>We do **not**</u>:

- Tell a person that their lack of faith is responsible if they don't get healed (although this is often true, it only creates guilt, doubt, and defensiveness which causes further difficulty in receiving healing), but rather encourage them to keep reading God's Word, seeking Jesus, and to return for continued prayer and ministry. Some healings are instant; some occur in degrees or as a gradual process.

- Advertise ourselves as counselors (in some places this is illegal if the worker does not possess the proper credentials, or as healers (we don't heal, only God does). What we do offer is teaching about Jesus and prayer.

- Tell anyone they should not take medicine or go to a doctor.

Have an exciting and comfortable environment. Be creative! You can decorate and provide a relevant atmosphere; i.e., Scriptures, banners or pictures of related healing scenes.

Important Note: Follow-up and responsibility for discipleship of those individuals who get born again, and/or healed at the Jesus Healing House can be funneled into your church, or another church if they live outside of your church's geographical area, to become a part of regular church life including fellowship, ministry, teaching, and other activities.

NEXT STEPS

➢ Host a Jesus Healing House Seminar as a community outreach. Bring the lost into your church for harvesting and ministry.

➢ Get your people involved! If you would like, we can coordinate plans for the Jesus Healing House seminar using church workers as greeter/ushers, worship team, and prayer ministers. For an all-out evangelistic effort, we can train and send teams door-to-door in your community to invite people to the event and to get to know your church.

➢ Seek God whether to establish a God's Glory Care Center as an integral part of your church's regular outreach and ministry program.

Establishing a God's Glory Care Center is a great opportunity to impact believers and your local community with the Gospel of Christ, which in turn will impact your city, state, nation and ultimately the world.

I believe we are on the verge of witnessing a mighty move of God's Spirit in denominational and mainline churches, who have not yet had the experience, Paul describes in 1 Corinthians, chapter two:

> *1 And I, brethren, when I came to you, did not come with excellence of speech or of wisdom, declaring to you the testimony of God.*
>
> *2 For I determined not to know anything among you except Jesus Christ and Him crucified.*

3 I was with you in weakness, in fear, and in much trembling.

4 And my speech and my preaching were not with persuasive words of human wisdom, but in demonstration of the Spirit and of power,

5 that your faith should not be in the wisdom of men but in the power of God.

(1 Corinthians 2:1-5, NKJV)

We are living in strategic, critical times where people can no longer turn to the things they have depended on for support and safety in the past. There may come a time when hospitals are not available, government assistance is not available, and "business as usual" will not meet their needs. Believers and unbelievers alike will have to learn to trust God for their very survival. Jesus Healing House can be a lifeline through sharing the Gospel confirmed by signs, wonders, and miracles.

God has healed me supernaturally many times; that's why I am so excited about telling people about His healing ways and power! God is no respecter of persons; He will heal you just as He has healed me and many others.

I remember one of my earliest healing experiences: I injured my back at work, and the doctors then discovered that my spine had deteriorated. It was a mess…Off work for three months, I laid flat on my back, much of the time on the hard floor because that seemed to be least painful. The doctor suggested possible surgery but wasn't very optimistic about the outcome. I was a new Christian and had just heard about God's divine healing power, so I "hobbled" slowly over to the church which was located just a couple doors from the apartment building where I lived. The pastor and his assistant prayed for me and anointed me with oil as described in the book of James. Wow! The pain instantly disappeared! I literally "ran" home rejoicing. I bent over, swung my arms up and around and jumped up and down. No pain, no stiffness…I was completely healed! I went back to the doctor and he agreed that it was a miracle and I needed no further treatment. To God be the glory!

Many times in the Bible, it says concerning the people who witnessed Jesus' miracles: "And they marveled and glorified God." Doing the works of Jesus today is still the key to attaining the glory of God! Jesus considered miracles so important that He said they prove that He is who He says He is:

> *Believe Me that I am in the Father and the Father in Me; or else believe Me for the sake of the [very] works themselves. [If you cannot trust Me, at least let these works that I do in My Father's name convince you.]*
>
> (John 14:11 AMP)

Chapter Eight

The Destiny of Islam:
The End-time Role of the Muslim
in Today's World

This chapter is taken from *The Destiny of Islam in the End Times* written by Faisal Malick and published by Destiny Image Publishers.

(Materials from The Destiny of Islam in the End Times, by Faisal Malick, copyright 2008, used by permission of Destiny Image Publishers, 167 Walnut Bottom Road, Shippensburg, PA 17257 www.destinyimage.com)

Faisal Malick is a former devoted Muslim who believed that Jesus was a teacher, but certainly not the Son of God. After attempting to convert Christians to Islam, Faisal had an unexpected, life-changing encounter with the living God.

In *The Destiny of Islam in the End Times*, Faisal speaks to both the Christian and the Muslim from a vast experience and understanding of both faiths. The following is excerpted from Faisal's book:

233

Who Is Ishmael?

Today 1.6 billion Muslims stand at center stage, while the world watches and wonders. Israel warns of terrorism, the Church is watching the clock, and the people of Islam are seeking a revolution.

Muhammad, prophet of Islam, was a direct descendent of Ishmael through his second son, Kedar. Muhammad received revelations from an angel whom he believed to be Gabriel. These revelations later became the book of the Muslims, known as the Qur'an. Muslims believe that Abraham took his firstborn, Ishmael, to the altar of sacrifice on the mount instead of Isaac to substantiate Ishmael as the seed through which the whole earth would be blessed. The Muslims also believe that Muhammad was the fulfillment of God's promise to Abraham and that Muhammad was the prophet like unto Moses. They consider the Bible to be changed and not entirely authentic. The nation of Islam comes forth from Ishmael's descendent, Muhammad. So Islam's roots trace back to Ishmael, Abraham's first son.

Ishmael, around the age of 15, was cast out with his mother Hagar into the wilderness. Let's see what happens:

> *15 And the water was spent in the bottle, and she cast the child under one of the shrubs.*
>
> *16 And she went, and sat her down over against him a good way off, as it were a bow shot: for she said, Let me not see the death of the child. And she sat over against him, and lift up her voice, and wept.*

17 And God heard the voice of the lad; and the angel of God called to Hagar out of heaven, and said unto her, What aileth thee, Hagar? fear not; for God hath heard the voice of the lad where he is.

18 Arise, lift up the lad, and hold him in thine hand; for I will make him a great nation.

19 And God opened her eyes, and she saw a well of water; and she went, and filled the bottle with water, and gave the lad drink.

20 And God was with the lad; and he grew, and dwelt in the wilderness, and became an archer.

21 And he dwelt in the wilderness of Paran: and his mother took him a wife out of the land of Egypt.

(Genesis 21:15-21)

Ishmael wandered in the wilderness with Hagar and ran out of water. After being cast out of his father's house, he found himself dying in the wilderness under a shrub. Hagar could not look upon the pain of her dying son. In hopelessness, she left her son under a bush and walked away, crying out to God. She could not bear seeing her son die. All she could do was weep and cry out in her pain. All the while, the young boy himself lay dying under a bush.

Ishmael went from being a son (of Abraham) to a servant—his identity lay in conflict, his father image forever shattered.

The young lad was not just physically dying, but his heart was already broken with rejection and his soul pierced with sorrow. In a moment, he went from being a son to merely a servant. "Who am I...the son of a patriarch, the father of many nations, or just the son of a servant?" His identity lay in conflict, and his image of a father was forever shattered. To make matters worse, at the door of death in the wilderness, his own mother left him to die alone. His condition was so bad that his mother could not look at him.

Ishmael was brought up learning about God from his father Abraham; but stranded in the desert, he must have been wondering where his God was. Had God forsaken and forgotten about him? The Bible says that God heard the voice of the lad and knew where he was (see Genesis 21:17). Notice God did not hear the mother but the boy, in the very place he was—the place of death, pain, rejection, and thirst.

God heard the lad because *Ishmael* means "God hears." God knew the end from the beginning; He named Ishmael before he was born because of the plan and destiny for his life. God heard his cry in the wilderness and opened the eyes of Hagar so she could see a well of water and give Ishmael water to drink that he might live. Amazingly, the well was already there, but they could not see it.

The Cry of Ishmael

Four thousand years later, the Muslim people are in a spiritual wilderness, with a cry that has deepened; they are dying of thirst, unable to see the well of their salvation. But God is going to hear the cry of Ishmael and open his eyes and show him the well of living water—Jesus—that he may drink and live. It took water to save his natural life, and it will take living water from the well of Jesus to save his spiritual life.

The hour has come for the Muslim people to see Jesus and know the Father. We as a Church must discern the times we are living in and hear the sound of Heaven. We must intercede for the Muslims like a mother would for her dying child. Some of us have walked away from Ishmael, just like his own mother did, because the condition of Ishmael seems so hopeless in many ways; but we must yield to the Spirit of God and pray that God will awaken the cry that is in the hearts of the Muslim people and stir it so deeply that it touches the heart of the Most High.

God will hear the cry of the Muslim people in this hour. God named Ishmael before he was born, in His wisdom, because one day he knew there would be 1.6 billion Muslims in a spiritual wilderness. Church, get ready—an entire generation of Muslims is going to come into the Kingdom. I believe that all of a sudden, 800 million to 1 billion Muslims will enter the Kingdom of God.

The Islam Religion

Centuries later, the children of Ishmael built a memorial around the cry of Ishmael and called it *Islam,* which means to submit to God much like a servant, rather than to have a relationship with him as a son. Islam filled the void of his heart, saying God is not a Father and has no Son. Islam became the face of God to Ishmael. Muslims still see themselves as servants or slaves submitting to God, hoping that, through their works, they can obtain acceptance and approval from God and avoid inevitable judgment. They seek to earn acceptance by God through works rather than grace. This is not just a moral code but the state of being of every Muslim. Regardless, the cry of Ishmael has never ceased but has deepened with time.

Islam fills the void of a fatherless heart.

Today the Muslim people continue in this wilderness at the point of death. Once again, in this spiritual wilderness, there is a well that they cannot see. They have no father to give them bread or water. At the same time, the Church is walking away from them, unable to watch them die.

God is calling out to the Muslim people in this hour. He will hear their cry and open their eyes and show them the face of Jesus in the well of living water of the glory of God. God will be their Father and give their hungry souls fresh bread from Heaven and their thirsty hearts living water that they may live. God is going to manifest His glory among Ishmael and revive him in the presence of Jesus.

The Father is going to give an identity to the Muslim people in this hour. He will reveal to them the truth about their destiny hidden in the name of Ishmael. He will show them His covenant and give them an inheritance in Christ Jesus. He will never leave them nor forsake them. Rather, this archer, Ishmael, once born of the Spirit will become an arrow in the bow of God's hand shot right into the heart of the enemy that once blinded him.

Terrorism and Islam
The Spirit of Esau

There is an element of terrorism and war within the Muslim world today. This particular element is at the center of the world's stage. With all the television and media coverage, it is a difficult subject to ignore. Some countries are concerned about the rapid growth of Muslim populations within their borders, for fear of potential Islamic fundamentalism. Dormant cells of fundamentalists are scattered across the Western world, leaving much concern for a new enemy from within.

Following are the biblical insights about Esau, then Ishmael and Esau, and their connection to terrorism.

Rebekah (in the Bible), Isaac's wife, was the mother of Esau and Jacob. She was pregnant with twins, and even before birth, these two nations struggled with one another in her womb. She went to ask the Lord about all this:

> *And the children struggled together within her; and she said, If it be so, why am I thus? And she went to enquire of the LORD. And the LORD said unto her, Two nations are in thy womb, and two manner of people shall be separated from thy bowels; and the one people shall be stronger than the other people; and the elder shall serve the younger.*

> (Genesis 25:22-23)

Esau was to serve the younger, though contrary to normal tradition and culture. Two very differently natured people were separated from her womb, and Esau became stronger than Jacob. Today, the people of Esau are stronger than the people of Jacob.

> *And the boys grew: and Esau was a cunning*
> *hunter, a man of the field; and Jacob was a*
> *plain man, dwelling in tents.*
>
> (Genesis 25:27)

Esau grew up a skilled hunter; he was a man of the wild. Esau was a strong man; his descendants would be much like him.

Esau's Birthright and Jacob's Blessing

Esau sold his birthright for a bowl of soup. He came in tired from the field and begged Jacob for some "red pottage" (see Genesis 25:30). Esau despised his birthright and sold it for a bowl of lentils and bread (see Genesis 25:31-34).

Isaac was getting old, and his eyes were dim. He wanted to pass on the blessing of Abraham to his eldest son, Esau, before he died. So Isaac sent him out to hunt some game and prepare food for him so he could eat it and bless Esau:

> *Now therefore take, I pray thee, thy weapons,*
> *thy quiver and thy bow, and go out to the field,*
> *and take me some venison; And make me*
> *savoury meat, such as I love, and bring it to*

*me, that I may eat; that my soul may bless thee
before I die.*

(Genesis 27:3-4)

Rebekah overheard Isaac and told Jacob to fetch some
meat, so that she could make the food for Isaac, in order
that Jacob could receive the blessing from Isaac instead of
Esau. She devised a plan to dress Jacob with Esau's clothes
so that he would smell like Esau. She also covered his arms
and neck with goat hair so that Jacob would seem as hairy
as Esau (see Genesis 27:14, 17). The plan worked, and
Isaac blessed Jacob and gave him the blessing of Abraham.

Esau came home with his hunted game and cooked a
meal for his father, Isaac; only to find out that Jacob had
already received the blessing. Esau wept and begged Isaac
for any additional blessing for himself. Isaac could not
give him the blessing of Abraham or the blessing of the
firstborn, but Isaac answered Esau:

*And by thy sword shalt thou live, and shalt
serve thy brother; and it shall come to pass
when thou shalt have the dominion, that thou
shalt break his yoke from off thy neck.*

(Genesis 27:40)

Esau hated Jacob because of the blessing that Isaac
blessed Jacob with. Esau sold his birthright to Jacob and
also lost the blessing of his birthright. Esau now planned in
his heart to kill Jacob (see Genesis 27:41).

Jacob became Israel. Even today, Esau hates Israel. Esau does live by the sword, and Esau's descendents are a people stronger than Israel. Esau has always been at war with Jacob. The struggle that began in their mother's womb continues. Jacob grabbed hold of Esau's heel when he was born, and ever since, Esau has believed he will crush Jacob under his heel.

Esau went to Ishmael, his uncle, and married his daughter, Mahalath. Ever since then, Esau and Ishmael have been mingled together in covenant…Esau lived by the sword, and Ishmael was always at war.

My intent is not to focus on the literal blood descendents of Esau, for God loves the descendents of Esau the same as all people on the face of the earth. However we must gain insight into the spirit or nature of Esau to understand why God is exposing the face of terrorism in Islam today.

There are two groups of people among Islam today, those who have the cry of Ishmael in their hearts and those who have the intent of Esau in their hearts. I'm not talking about Sunni or Shiias, I'm talking about two types of hearts among the Muslim people. One group is the majority of Muslims, with the cry of Ishmael in their hearts. This cry is the longing to be accepted and loved by a father, to have an inheritance, to find blessing from the father, and to find approval and an inheritance. This is the heart and the cry of the majority of the Muslim people today. They see terrorism and realize that Islam has not answered the cry of their own hearts. They are still hungry and thirsty in a spiritual wilderness, looking for God to respond to the crisis in Islam.

Ishmael's cry and Esau's pain
that once united, now divides.

The other group is comprised of Muslims who have embraced the spirit of Esau and have sold their natural birthright to terrorism, with no regard for life. They are willing to strap a bomb around their chest and die in the hope of waking up in paradise with 72 virgins. This spirit is not interested in peace, but in terrorism until death. This spirit has been around for generations. This group includes the terrorists and those who favor them. Thankfully this group is the minority.

The Bible Cure for Terrorism

For we wrestle not against flesh and blood, but against principalities, against powers, against the rulers of the darkness of this world, against spiritual wickedness in high places.

(Ephesians 6:12)

I learned a long time ago that the plans of the Spirit are birthed into this realm through prayer. God's Word is forever settled in Heaven but must be established on earth. We, as a people, must pray out the plan of God to be established on the earth. We must take authority over the spirit of Esau through prayer. When we pray, God exposes the deceitful strategies of the enemy and makes a way for His purposes to be established. Just as watchmen watch a city, so in the Kingdom, watchmen watch and pray in the Spirit against all principalities and powers, and can see what the enemy is trying to do and intercede for those in danger.

The Destiny of Islam Today

Today, when God hears the cry of Ishmael, He will use the Church to give him water from the well of everlasting life. It took water to save his life from death in the wilderness. Today it will take living water to save him from death unto life eternal. God is going to use the conversion of Ishmael to stir up the Church, as God used the conversion of Saul to stir up the early Church in the midst of persecution.

God will use Ishmael to provoke the Church into a passion for Jesus—what the Church has forsaken, Ishmael will embrace. God is going to use Ishmael to provoke Israel to jealousy for the Messiah.

After being cast out of Abraham's house, the last time Ishmael saw his father was to bury him. And that was the last time that Ishmael and Isaac came together. Ever since that time they have been separated—until now. It was the *death* of a father that separated them. Now it will be the *revelation* of the Father that will bring them back together again—and there will be a family reunion in Christ Jesus.

Ishmael's Cry Will Be Heard

God loves the Muslim people. I (Faisal Malick) am a living example—I was a Muslim. I'm so grateful. All my life, I never imagined or dreamed that I'd know Jesus as the Son of God. As a Muslim, that thought never crossed my mind. I remember walking the streets of Pakistan as a young man, wondering...*Lord, is there even a purpose for my life, any reason I need to live?*

God Loves Muslims.

The Truth

(To my Muslim friends): I hope that this reading is giving you spiritually deep thoughts that prompt you to search yourself to find the Spirit of God resident inside you. I hope you find Christ, the Son of God, and the Spirit of God revealing Himself to you. I pray you find the person of Jesus who redeemed all people as He died on the cross to prove the Word is true. I pray that you have a revelation of the Father sitting on the throne welcoming you to Himself.

The Word of God bears fruit in your life according to His purpose and plan for your life. If it's bearing fruit; that is another witness. The Word is a person and a real relationship. Jesus said the Scriptures testify and reveal Him and are a revelation of a person. That's why Jesus said, *"I AM the truth, I AM the way and I AM the life"* (John 14:6).

(Please read the next chapter for more revelation on Jesus and heaven.)

Muslim Wealth and Ishmael's Blessing

God is raising up apostles and prophets in these last days who will have their own oil wells to deliver the

Word of the Lord. They will have the financial resources to establish God's covenant on the earth. God will give creative ideas to the Body of Christ that will position believers in places of financial dominion in times of famine in the world. There will be a dominion anointing to function in the marketplace that will marvel skeptics in the business world. God is about to bring many into a wealthy place so they can fund the greatest harvest ever.

God is not going to place the command of such wealth into the hands of people who do not know their purpose in the Kingdom. It is necessary to know the purpose for which you were created and to recognize the gift that is within you to fulfill your destiny. Revelation of purpose precedes the manifestation of provision.

> *But thou shalt remember the LORD thy God:*
> *for it is he that giveth thee power to get*
> *wealth, that he may establish his covenant*
> *which he sware unto thy fathers, as it is this*
> *day.*
>
> (Deuteronomy 8:18)

God gives us the power to get wealth, but we must not forget that it is for the purpose of establishing His covenant on the earth. This is the same covenant that God made with Abraham to bless all the families of the earth through his seed whom we know as the Lord Jesus Christ.

God's Purpose in Blessing Ishmael

We know God's works are clothed with purpose. God's provision is always hidden in His blessing. I (Faisal

246

Malick) would like to share with you the role of Ishmael in the end-time wealth transfer:

> *And as for Ishmael, I have heard thee: Behold, I have blessed him, and will make him fruitful, and will multiply him exceedingly; twelve princes shall he beget, and I will make him a great nation.*

(Genesis 17:20)

Ishmael was deprived of the blessing of Abraham and any inheritance when he was cast out in the wilderness with his mother Hagar. But God did bless Ishmael with an unconditional blessing; and as a result, this blessing has accumulated and wealth has been stored up in the Muslim world. The Middle East alone provides more than half of the world's oil.

For years, Ishmael's oil wells have been storing up wealth in the Muslim world that has spilled into the commerce and the business communities worldwide. They are very careful to support other Muslim businesses first, much like the Jewish communities. Muslims are forbidden in the Qur'an to charge interest, and Muslim lending organizations do not charge interest to other Muslims on mortgages and loans. This way, their homes are paid off more quickly. They accumulate more equity in their homes, and they can invest in more property.

They believe in owning land, property, and real estate wherever they settle. The Muslim people have been zealous about both their religious and their economic dominions. There is an enormous amount of wealth that has been stored up for thousands of years in the Muslim world, and it is still being stored up today. From the earliest days on, the Ishmaelites were businessmen who traded in the marketplace with caravans of goods. Commerce was a way of life for them. This wealth has been stored up for a purpose.

Provision for His purpose is hidden in His blessing.

God blessed Ishmael thousands of years ago, knowing that when he would come into the Kingdom, the treasure hidden in dark places and the secret treasure that is stored up will come into the Kingdom to finance the Gospel in part. Even the oil in the wells will be for the Gospel's sake. He has provision for His purpose hidden in His blessing.

I believe that God blessed Ishmael unconditionally with the intention to fund the end-time harvest in part. We will see enormous wealth transfer from the Muslim world in the billions and trillions. God preserved the oil and raw materials in the earth for resources to establish His covenant. He created the earth in its fullness and all that is in the earth belongs to Him. God gives the power to get wealth for the sole purpose of establishing His covenant in the end times.

The Glory and the Gold

Arise, shine; for thy light is come, and the glory of the LORD is risen upon thee. For, behold, the darkness shall cover the earth, and gross darkness the people: but the LORD shall arise upon thee, and his glory shall be seen upon thee. And the Gentiles shall come to thy light, and kings to the brightness of thy rising.

(Isaiah 60:1-3)

As we study the Scriptures, we see the glory of God coming upon the Church and the manifestation of His glory causing nations and kings to come into the Kingdom.

Then thou shalt see, and flow together, and thine heart shall fear, and be enlarged; because the abundance of the sea shall be converted unto thee, the forces of the Gentiles shall come unto thee. The multitude of camels shall cover thee, the dromedaries of Midian and Ephah; all they from Sheba shall come: they shall bring gold and incense; and they shall shew forth the praises of the LORD. All the flocks of Kedar shall be gathered together unto thee, the rams of Nebaioth shall minister unto thee: they shall come up with acceptance on mine altar, and I will glorify the house of my glory.

(Isaiah 60:5-7)

According to Scripture, the wealth and treasure of the Gentiles will come into the Kingdom. Muslims represent 42 percent of the Gentiles today. In verses 6 and 7, we see a description of the forces of the Gentiles that will come into our hands. Kedar was the second son of Ishmael and ancestor to Mohammed, the prophet of Islam. The Scripture says that all the flocks of Kedar, speaking of the people and the wealth and substance of Ishmael, will transfer into the Kingdom. Muslims have always directed their wealth toward their religious beliefs—the expansion of Islam through the building of mosques and so on. When their eyes are opened, they will catch the vision of God's heart and continue to passionately support the Gospel. I believe that when Ishmael is revived in the presence of God, he will lay his treasures at the feet of Jesus and embrace his destiny.

(Author's Note): Space herein allows only a small portion of Faisal Malick's book *The Destiny of Islam in the End Times.* If you would like to order this timely, exciting book in its entirety, please visit Faisal's website: www.covenantoflife.org, contact the publisher at www.destinyimage.com, or visit your local bookstore.

Chapter Nine

Departing for Heaven at "Gate Jesus": Don't Miss Your Departure Time!

There have been reports from all over the world about people having dreams and visions of Jesus, especially in countries that are closed to the Gospel. One man from Mississippi shared that he had a dream one night about his mother who had been deceased for four years. She was dressed all in white, shining, beaming, about the same age as when she died, but looking her best. She said to him, "Son, you must study (the Bible). Jesus is coming soon!"

In the Bible are multiple references to the kingdom of heaven. The powerful message of John the Baptist, the forerunner of Jesus, plus Jesus Himself declared boldly, "Repent for the kingdom of heaven is at hand." This message has not changed today, but has taken on even more urgency and significance as the time draws ever nearer. The world is standing on the very threshold of eternity. The Scripture warns that many will be unaware that Jesus is coming soon for His Church, and God's judgments will soon permeate the earth.

Friend, you must be ready if you want to escape the coming horrific tribulation and enter into the kingdom of heaven with Jesus.

Jesus shared numerous parables about the kingdom of heaven with His followers and the people of His day. Parables make use of everyday, common activities and knowledge that were familiar to the people during the times in which they were told. These parables are recorded for us today, too, so that we can be forewarned and forearmed, recognizing the signs of the times. Pray, and ask God to show you the meaning of the following popular parable so that you might have understanding of how it personally fits your life and what He is saying to you. Heed also the warning to be ready for the kingdom of heaven for we do not know the day or the hour that Jesus will return for His own.

> *1 THEN THE kingdom of heaven shall be likened to ten virgins who took their lamps and went to meet the bridegroom.*
>
> *2 Five of them were foolish (thoughtless, without forethought) and five were wise (sensible, intelligent, and prudent).*
>
> *3 For when the foolish took their lamps, they did not take any [extra] oil with them;*
>
> *4 But the wise took flasks of oil along with them [also] with their lamps.*
>
> *5 While the bridegroom lingered and was slow in coming, they all began nodding their heads, and they fell asleep.*

6 But at midnight there was a shout, Behold, the bridegroom! Go out to meet him!

7 Then all those virgins got up and put their own lamps in order.

8 And the foolish said to the wise, Give us some of your oil, for our lamps are going out.

9 But the wise replied, There will not be enough for us and for you; go instead to the dealers and buy for yourselves.

10 But while they were going away to buy, the bridegroom came, and those who were prepared went in with him to the marriage feast; and the door was shut.

11 Later the other virgins also came and said, Lord, Lord, open [the door] to us!

12 But He replied, I solemnly declare to you, I do not know you [I am not acquainted with you].

13 Watch therefore [give strict attention and be cautious and active], for you know neither the day nor the hour when the Son of Man will come.

(Matthew 25:1-13, AMP)

Jesus unexpectedly appears to Paul

Many report actual visitations from Jesus like the Apostle Paul experienced in the Bible:

12 "On one of these journeys I was going to Damascus with the authority and commission of the chief priests.

253

13 About noon, O king, as I was on the road, I saw a light from heaven, brighter than the sun, blazing around me and my companions.

14 We all fell to the ground, and I heard a voice saying to me in Aramaic, 'Saul, Saul, why do you persecute me? It is hard for you to kick against the goads.'

15 "Then I asked, 'Who are you, Lord?'

" 'I am Jesus, whom you are persecuting,' the Lord replied.

16 'Now get up and stand on your feet. I have appeared to you to appoint you as a servant and as a witness of what you have seen of me and what I will show you.

(Acts 26:12-16, NIV)

The highway to hell is broad—and many will choose it!

Many people will choose the easy way. They are filled with pride, deception, the allure of sin, and even their own human intellect that scorns the idea of heaven and hell. Do not be complacent or overconfident! There is only one Way to God's kingdom…through the narrow gate. This Word from God requires you to make a decision that will affect you for all of eternity. We cannot put it off until tomorrow. My friend, if I were to ask you, "If you died today, do you know if you would go to heaven," what would you say? You may not be sick or on your deathbed today, but there is no guarantee for tomorrow. We are living in an uncertain world where life can be snuffed out in an instant. So, keep reading and you will discover what you need to do to enter in the narrow gate to God's kingdom.

"You can enter God's Kingdom only through the narrow gate. The highway to hell is broad, and its gate is wide for the many who choose that way. But the gateway to life is very narrow and the road is difficult, and only a few ever find it.

(Matthew 7:13-14, NLT)

Why would anyone choose hell instead of heaven?

Why would anyone choose to spend eternity in the horrible, blazing hot inferno called "hell?" I don't think anyone in their right mind would make this choice knowingly. You've heard the expression "misery loves company?" The devil has but a short time left before he gets cast into hell, his permanent home since trying to overthrow the throne of God, so he wants to bring as many people with him as he can! The devil deceives humanity into thinking there is no heaven and there is no hell; therefore, people feel they can live their lives in any way that "feels good" to them without regard to consequences. What a tragedy for those who turn their back on Jesus and choose to follow the devil!

Jesus came to earth to recover man's soul from the devil and restore his relationship with God. He promises a life of peace and eternal joy for those who choose to follow Him rather than the "deceiver." My friend, there is a real place called heaven, and many people, who have had near-death experiences, have come back to life to share what they saw and heard in heaven. Their descriptions closely align with what the Bible tells us, and give further hope that heaven is a real place, which means also that the Bible is true in what it says about hell, and this too is a real place.

Included in chapter two of this book was a brief description of heaven, and here we expand upon that. Following is the vision of heaven shown to the Apostle John that he might write it down to bring true hope to believers of all ages. Be encouraged that whatever you may have suffered on earth, you have an eternal destiny that will wipe away your tears and pain and bring you into a place of unbelievable beauty and blissful serenity. Take a look with me now at our future home:

10 So he took me in the Spirit to a great, high mountain, and he showed me the holy city, Jerusalem, descending out of heaven from God.

11 It shone with the glory of God and sparkled like a precious stone—like jasper as clear as crystal.

12 The city wall was broad and high, with twelve gates guarded by twelve angels. And the names of the twelve tribes of Israel were written on the gates.

13 There were three gates on each side—east, north, south, and west.

14 The wall of the city had twelve foundation

stones, and on them were written the names of the twelve apostles of the Lamb.

15 The angel who talked to me held in his hand a gold measuring stick to measure the city, its gates, and its wall.

16 When he measured it, he found it was a square, as wide as it was long. In fact, its length and width and height were each 1,400 miles.

17 Then he measured the walls and found them to be 216 feet thick (according to the human standard used by the angel).

18 The wall was made of jasper, and the city was pure gold, as clear as glass.

19 The wall of the city was built on foundation stones inlaid with twelve precious stones: the first was jasper, the second sapphire, the third agate, the fourth emerald,

20 the fifth onyx, the sixth carnelian, the seventh chrysolite, the eighth beryl, the ninth topaz, the tenth chrysoprase, the eleventh jacinth, the twelfth amethyst.

21 The twelve gates were made of pearls— each gate from a single pearl! And the main street was pure gold, as clear as glass.

22 I saw no temple in the city, for the Lord God Almighty and the Lamb are its temple.

23 And the city has no need of sun or moon, for the glory of God illuminates the city, and the Lamb is its light.

(Revelation 21:10-23, NLT)

Don't fear suffering—you have a glorious reward!

In these end times, there may be fierce persecution and attacks on the Christian Church. Government authorities, religious authorities, unbelievers in every walk of life will come against the Church, calling it "intolerant," and believing that they are doing the right thing by hunting down Christians, arresting them, and even killing some.

God will take care of His children who are patiently waiting for Him. We have God's faithful promises of blessing and protection upon which to base our faith for the remaining days of our journey upon this earth. And, even more importantly, we have a glorious promise of hope for eternity.

> *And now the prize awaits me—the crown of righteousness, which the Lord, the righteous Judge, will give me on the day of his return. And the prize is not just for me but for all who eagerly look forward to his appearing.*

> (2 Timothy 4:8, NLT)

Whether God performs incredible miracles of escape, protection, provision and supernatural supply like Jesus did when He fed over 5,000 men plus an untold number of women and children with only two loaves of bread and five fishes…whether God sovereignly heals your body from disease or inflicted wounds…or chooses to call you home to be with Him forever, we have to be ready for whatever comes upon the earth. In some cases, this may be suffering, even martyrdom for the cause of Christ.

Even though we always want to believe for the best, if we are not prepared for what could happen, we may weaken and fail in our faith toward Christ or decide that it's just too hard to stand for Jesus. Above all things, we must endure—we must stand firm until the end. An eternity spent in hell is too big a price to pay for a short time of anguish in our earthly flesh.

> *So be truly glad. There is wonderful joy ahead, even though you have to endure many trials for a little while. These trials will show that your faith is genuine. It is being tested as fire tests and purifies gold—though your faith is far more precious than mere gold. So when your faith remains strong through many trials, it will bring you much praise and glory and honor on the day when Jesus Christ is revealed to the whole world.*
>
> (1 Peter 5:6-7, NLT)

Jesus suffered in the flesh…in His human form, when all the sins in the entire world were placed upon Him. The struggle was so great that He sweat drops of blood in the garden of Gethsemane. Jesus suffered excruciating pain and humiliation hanging on that cross at Calvary, paying the price of redemption for you and for me. If you watched Mel Gibson's movie production, *The Passion of the Christ,* you will have a small idea of the suffering that Jesus endured!

Jesus has overcome the world!

Jesus, our example and our strength, is a conqueror, an overcomer of every worldly evil.

> *I have told you these things, so that in Me*
> *you may have [perfect] peace and confidence.*
> *In the world you have tribulation and trials*
> *and distress and frustration; but be of good*
> *cheer [take courage; be confident, certain,*
> *undaunted]! For I have overcome the world.*
> *[I have deprived it of power to harm you and*
> *have conquered it for you.]*
>
> (John 16:33, AMP)

Few are called to go through suffering like Jesus did, though many in the early church and even in countries today, where the Gospel is not allowed and people are greatly persecuted, have also experienced such atrocities.

But, do not walk in fear, my brother and my sister; Jesus has promised to make a way of escape and will give you the strength, in His power, to overcome.

God is calling you to be a conqueror, an overcomer! Through Jesus Christ, who lives in you, you will have the grace and peace to stand against all of the temptations and attacks of our enemy, the devil, the one who is "in the world."

> *Little children, you are of God [you belong*
> *to Him] and have [already] defeated and*

overcome them [the agents of the antichrist],
because He Who lives in you is greater
(mightier) than he who is in the world.

(1 John 4:4, AMP)

Your faith—God-given and God sustained—will bring the sweet joy of victory! The joy of the Lord is your strength (See Nehemiah 8:10). Spend time with Jesus…in prayer… in praise…in just being still, listening for His gentle voice. Jesus in you is your hope of glory and your power to live a victorious life now and forever. Stay strong, my friend… you are called to win the battle not only for yourself, but for all those that God would send across your path that need to know the way to eternal life.

For every child of God defeats this evil world,
and we achieve this victory through our
faith. And who can win this battle against the
world? Only those who believe that Jesus is
the Son of God.

(1 John 5:4-5, NLT)

You can overcome!

"How do we overcome?" you ask. The key for overcoming the devil, who is the mastermind behind sin, sickness, and every other evil in the world, is found in the book of Revelation:

And they have defeated him by the blood of the
Lamb and by their testimony. And they did not

261

*love their lives so much that they were afraid
to die.*

(Revelation 12:11, NLT)

What are the three ways in which we overcome?

(1) We overcome through the blood of the Lamb.
Jesus Christ's finished work on the cross at
Calvary bought and paid for the forgiveness of
our sin. The devil can no longer accuse us of
anything. Our sins, weaknesses and failures are
covered by the blood of Jesus! This is the same
way we overcome sickness, disease, fear, anxiety
and any other thing that comes from the pit of
hell. Jesus paid it all, and we are free! (See John
19:30; Isaiah 53:4, 5; Galatians 3:13; Revelation
12:10.)

(2) We overcome through the word of our testimony.
This means, in the broadest sense, our testimony
of faith in Jesus Christ. However, there is great
power in what we believe and in the words we use
to express our beliefs. Speaking forth faith-filled,
victorious words can raise the level of our faith,
penetrating the situation with life, hope, and an
overcoming testimony. (See Proverbs 18:21; Mark
11:23, 24.)

(3) We overcome when we "love not our lives unto
the death." When our commitment to Christ
(through the strength given to us by His Spirit) is
so strong that we are willing to die for Him rather
than to deny Him, there is nothing left that the
devil can do to us! (See Revelation 12:11.)

*And when this perishable puts on the
imperishable and this that was capable of
dying puts on freedom from death, then shall
be fulfilled the Scripture that says, Death is
swallowed up (utterly vanquished forever)
in and unto victory. O death, where is your
victory? O death, where is your sting? Now
sin is the sting of death, and sin exercises its
power [upon the soul] through [the abuse of]
the Law.*

(1 Corinthians 15:54-56, AMP)

Stay steadfast in prayer, attentive to the Word of God, and strong in faith!

What encouragement we find in knowing that Jesus lived as a human man upon the earth, though at the same time, He was still fully God. Yet, He experienced some of the same feelings and needs that we do. Jesus got hungry and thirsty like we do. He got tired and needed sleep like we do. Jesus even experienced the temptations of sin, yet never succumbed to weakness. God's Lamb that was to be sacrificed for the payment of the penalties for sin that we so richly deserve had to be blameless and without sin, so He could be accepted by God for the redemption of our sin.

In the Old Testament, human priests had to offer sacrifices to God again and again to cover not only the sin of the people, but their own sin as well. But, Jesus Christ paid the price with His own body once, and for all time, and for all people—as many as would receive Him as their Savior.

*For we do not have a High Priest Who is
unable to understand and sympathize and
have a shared feeling with our weaknesses
and infirmities and liability to the assaults of
temptation, but One Who has been tempted in
every respect as we are, yet without sinning.
Let us then fearlessly and confidently and
boldly draw near to the throne of grace (the
throne of God's unmerited favor to us sinners),
that we may receive mercy [for our failures]
and find grace to help in good time for every
need [appropriate help and well-timed help,
coming just when we need it].*

(Hebrews 4:15-16, AMP)

Answers to prayer come through our position in Christ
Jesus. Through Him, we enter into God's throne room of
grace to boldly ask Him for what we need. Because we
are born-again in Christ, His Spirit dwelling in us, we are
children of God. If you are a parent who shows love to your
children, how do they approach you? Do your children
cower in fear, expecting the worst, when they come to you
with a request? Or, do they believe they will receive a good
response from you? If you have been born again, God is
your Father, and you can approach Him with confidence,
knowing that He will take care of you, your family, and
everything you need.

Be of good courage! You are not alone in prayer. Not
only can you join together with your brothers and sisters in
the Lord, singly or in corporate prayer opportunities within
the church, there is Someone else who is praying for you!
Jesus! Jesus is your mighty prayer intercessor!

264

*...Christ Jesus, who died—more than that,
who was raised to life—is at the right hand of
God and is also interceding for us.*

(Romans 8:34, NIV)

How do you know if you are born again
and ready for heaven?

John, chapter three, is probably one of the most important chapters in the entire Bible. This is where Jesus explains what it means to be born again:

*1 There was a man named Nicodemus, a
Jewish religious leader who was a Pharisee.*

*2 After dark one evening, he came to speak
with Jesus. "Rabbi," he said, "we all know
that God has sent you to teach us. Your
miraculous signs are evidence that God is
with you."*

*3 Jesus replied, "I tell you the truth, unless
you are born again, you cannot see the
Kingdom of God."*

*4 "What do you mean?" exclaimed
Nicodemus. "How can an old man go back
into his mother's womb and be born again?"*

*5 Jesus replied, "I assure you, no one can
enter the Kingdom of God without being born
of water and the Spirit.*

*6 Humans can reproduce only human life, but
the Holy Spirit gives birth to spiritual life.*

*7 So don't be surprised when I say, 'You must
be born again.'*

8 The wind blows wherever it wants. Just as you can hear the wind but can't tell where it comes from or where it is going, so you can't explain how people are born of the Spirit."

9 "How are these things possible?" Nicodemus asked.

10 Jesus replied, "You are a respected Jewish teacher, and yet you don't understand these things?

11 I assure you, we tell you what we know and have seen, and yet you won't believe our testimony.

12 But if you don't believe me when I tell you about earthly things, how can you possibly believe if I tell you about heavenly things?

13 No one has ever gone to heaven and returned. But the Son of Man has come down from heaven.

14 And as Moses lifted up the bronze snake on a pole in the wilderness, so the Son of Man must be lifted up,

15 so that everyone who believes in him will have eternal life.

16 "For God loved the world so much that he gave his one and only Son, so that everyone who believes in him will not perish but have eternal life.

17 God sent his Son into the world not to judge the world, but to save the world through him.

*18 "There is no judgment against anyone
who believes in him. But anyone who does not
believe in him has already been judged for not
believing in God's one and only Son.*

*19 And the judgment is based on this fact:
God's light came into the world, but people
loved the darkness more than the light, for
their actions were evil.*

*20 All who do evil hate the light and refuse to
go near it for fear their sins will be exposed.*

*21 But those who do what is right come to
the light so others can see that they are doing
what God wants."*

(John 3:1-21, NLT)

Being born again is a spiritual experience wherein your spiritual eyes are opened to see and understand the things pertaining to God and eternal life. The Holy Spirit comes to live in you and to reveal truths about Jesus—your Savior—and Lord over every area of your life into which you will invite Him. In the Scripture portion above, Jesus told Nicodemus that he had to be born again; he had to enter into a personal relationship with Jesus Christ to attain God's promise of eternal life in heaven.

Even though Nicodemus was a respected religious leader, merely knowing about God and being religious wasn't enough to guarantee the salvation of his eternal soul. Some people think they're ok because they believe in God (mentally), go to church, or do good works. As admirable as these things may be, they will not save you.

How do you get saved—or born again? All you have to do is to realize and admit that you are a sinner and that you cannot save yourself or quit sinning in your own strength and ability. Then repent (change your mind), believe on the Lord Jesus Christ, and ask Him to come into your heart and life. You can ask this in your own words. The important thing is that you mean what you say with all your heart, because just saying empty words or going through the motions will only give you a false sense of hope, and you will neither see nor receive the life-changing experience you desire.

The only criteria for salvation is that you personally believe that Jesus died on the cross and paid the price for your sins, and that He was raised from the dead by God. If you, now or at some time in your life, have sincerely from your heart acknowledged that you have sinned, repented, and asked Jesus to be your Savior, the Bible says you are saved, born again, and have become a new creation in Christ Jesus. (John 3, Romans 10, 2 Corinthians 5:17)

Good works do not save anyone; rather they are the result of the work of the Holy Spirit in a person who has been born again through faith in Jesus Christ. (Ephesians 2:8, Galatians 5: 22). Sometimes, because of the stresses of life and the lies and temptations of the devil, we don't feel saved. But the Word of God is true, so we can confidently believe in what it says rather than what our feelings tell us.

How do you receive this wonderful gift of salvation through Jesus Christ?

"...If you confess with your mouth the Lord Jesus and believe in your heart that God has raised Him from the dead, you will be saved. For with the heart one believes unto righteousness, and with the mouth confession is made unto salvation."

(Romans 10:9-10, NKJV)

If you sincerely believe in your heart, all you need to do is ask Jesus to be your personal Savior and Lord. Use your own words, or you can pray something like this:

"Dear God,

I believe that Jesus Christ is Your Son, and that He died on the cross to pay the price for my sins. I also believe that You raised Him from the dead that I might have eternal life in Him. I repent of my sins and ask you to forgive me. Jesus, come into my heart; be my Savior and Lord. Help me live for You, and fulfill the wonderful plan God has for my life. Thank you, Lord, for saving me. I am a born again child of God. Amen."

Congratulations, my friend! If you have sincerely asked Jesus into your life, then you have become born again. You are forgiven! You now have access to the Father Himself! You can talk to Him and share your deepest thoughts and desires with Him any time you want. Your heavenly Father is always waiting to hear from you! The Word of God describes the wonderful experience into which you have just entered like this:

*Therefore, if anyone is in Christ, he is a
new creation; old things have passed away;
behold, all things have become new.*

(2 Corinthians 5:17, NKJV)

You have just embarked upon the exciting life of being a believer in Christ Jesus! Spend time talking with God every day (prayer), and finding out more about Him and His Son Jesus, (reading the Bible). You will grow as you attend a Bible-believing and preaching church and fellowship with other Christians. Praise the Lord! Welcome to the family of God! You are now His cherished son or daughter. Believe that your heavenly Father loves you dearly and will do good to you!

I encourage you to take any concerns you have to God in prayer, and continually, diligently study the Bible. In it, you will find the answers and hope that you need. Seek God through prayer, worship, and reading His Word for His perfect plan and provision for you and your family. He promises to meet all of your needs.

*"And my God shall supply all your need
according to His riches in glory by Christ
Jesus."*

(Philippians 4:19, NKJV)

Some things in your life will change immediately; but others may take time as you grow spiritually. Be patient with yourself and know that if you make a mistake or fall into an old sin (temporarily), you are eternally forgiven for past, present and future sins. God will not punish you or send bad things your way, but you may reap the results of your foolish words or actions if you choose not to repent and turn from your sin.

You can have a fresh start!

Don't stay in your sin! God has made a way out for you…a way to start fresh again:

> *If we [freely] admit that we have sinned and confess our sins, He is faithful and just (true to His own nature and promises) and will forgive our sins [dismiss our lawlessness] and [continuously] cleanse us from all unrighteousness [everything not in conformity to His will in purpose, thought, and action].*
>
> (1 John 1:9, AMP)

You can pray something like this:

> *"Father,*
>
> *Thank you for making me a new creation in Christ Jesus now that I am saved and born again into Your kingdom. I confess my sin of (name it) to You, knowing that Your mercies are new every morning and that You will forgive me. Give me strength to give up (name it) or to resist doing (name it) in the future. I thank you that I am forgiven and have a fresh start with You because You have cleansed my sin by the blood of Christ. In Jesus' Name, Amen."*

If you are already a believer...

Sometimes the greatest attacks and failures do not come from satan, but from within the Church...from fellow members of the body of Christ.

It is time to clean up corruption, complacency and compromise that exists in the Church today. God is revealing and reproving sin, calling us to repentance, and to a greater commitment to follow Jesus.

Are you being faithful to find and occupy your place of service for the Lord? Some believers are unwilling to do their part in their local church...serve in the nursery, as an usher, on the parking lot traffic team, or show up when the doors open for corporate prayer. They come to church to receive the benefit of a spiritual "feel good" high, a word from the Lord for the challenges they face, or a pat on the back for being a faithful attender. Some come strictly out of duty, feeling they have earned "brownie points" with God for that week.

In spite of all that may seem to be falling and failing around us, the believer who truly loves and obeys the Lord has an awesome promise from God:

> *Yet in all these things (trials, persecutions, temptations) we are more than conquerors through Him who loved us.*
>
> (Romans 8:37, NKJV)

It isn't by our strength or abilities that we will conquer and walk in victory, but through walking close with Jesus and yielding to His direction, strength and power:

I have strength for all things in Christ Who empowers me [I am ready for anything and equal to anything through Him Who infuses inner strength into me; I am self-sufficient in Christ's sufficiency].

(Philippians 4:13, AMP)

Soon, we will hear the trumpet call and Jesus will return for those who are His

Whether you have just become born again or have been a believer for years, you need to know, that you know, that you know you are ready to meet the Lord. If you haven't already done so, sincerely pray the prayers in this chapter.

If you need to be born again, re-read the book of John, chapter three, and ask Jesus to be your Savior and Lord. Seek God with all your heart and trust in Jesus for your eternal future. There is not much time left; Jesus is coming soon! It will be too late to get right with God when the trumpet sounds announcing Jesus' return, or if you leave this earth through death before that time. Do it now! Don't delay another day...we have no guarantees for tomorrow.

I heard a story about a young man, sitting in the back of the church scoffing and making fun of the preacher. The preacher gave an invitation to those in the church to repent and receive Jesus as Savior; some came forward, but this young man just got up and defiantly walked out of the church. Little did he know, as he stepped out into the night's cold air and crossed the street into the face of an oncoming vehicle, that this would be his last day on the earth...and his last opportunity to be saved. God is merciful to the 'nnnnth degree! He called to this young man, through the invitation of that preacher, to make the most important decision of his life...to receive Jesus Christ into his heart.

Friend, please don't make this same tragic, irreversible mistake. Ask Jesus to save you now and to walk with you all the rest of your life. Seek and follow His plan for your life. It's a good one; I can promise you that, because God knows everything about you, what makes you happy, and the very purpose for which He created you. Don't miss it!

Believer, make sure you are ready, too. You may already be born again, but be sure that you are living for Jesus, free from complacency and compromise, walking in all the fullness of God's wonderful plan and purpose for your life. When He returns, will He find you "drunk" with all the pleasures of this world, or will He be able to say:

> ... *'Well done, good and faithful servant; you were faithful over a few things, I will make you ruler over many things. Enter into the joy of your (Lord Jesus).*

(Matthew 25:21, NKJV)

If you have gotten off track...if worldly cares and temptations have crept in...if your love for Jesus isn't as exciting and intense as it once was, then repent. Ask God to forgive you and to make all things new and fresh in your life. Give all of yourself...your dreams...your fears... and your needs to Him once again. Turn to the promise of forgiveness from God in your Bible (1 John 1:9), or re-read the previous section where this Scripture is also shown (page 271).

And, pray with me the following prayer (or use your own words) if you mean it from your heart:

"Father,

I confess to you that I haven't been living as I should and I want to change now. Please forgive me and set me free from (name it) through the shed blood of Jesus, my Savior and Lord. Thank you that you are faithful to forgive me as Your Word says, and to cleanse me from all unrighteousness. I receive Your divine strength and power to stay true to you and walk in your goodness all the days of my life. I am looking up and waiting for the appearing of my Lord Jesus. I am ready for His return! Help me Father to fully give myself to You and to Your plan and purpose for which You have created and equipped me. In Jesus' Name, Amen."

Praise the Lord, all of you whose hope is in Christ. There is a glorious, never-ending future awaiting you and me…in a place of unbelievable beauty, peace and joy…a place with no more tears, strife or failure…no more denominations, no more races, just God's people all together, worshiping Him and enjoying the things He has prepared for us for all eternity!

Holly Lewerenz

God's Glory Care Centers ♥ *An outreach of Jesus Healing House Ministries*

P.O. Box 31883 • Chicago, IL 60631

Phone: at (817) 285-0058 • *Email:* Holly@HealingforAmerica.com

Dear Pastor,

I hope that after reading this book, including chapter seven *Especially for Pastors: A Message and Model*, and hearing from the Spirit of the Lord, you have decided to begin a God's Glory Care Center in your church, or along with other pastors and churches, in your community. On page 197, there is a chart describing the four components of a God's Glory Care Center, which can be done individually or in conjunction with each other.

I would love to hear from you…if I can be of service in the areas of organizing, implementing, training, providing curriculum and administrative materials or any other assistance in getting your God's Glory Care Center off the ground!

Please feel free to email me at Holly@HealingforAmerica.com, or call me at (817) 285-0058. Or visit our website at www.JesusHealingHouse.org.

Sincerely,
Holly Lewerenz
Jesus Healing House Ministries

At God's Glory Care Centers

An outreach of Jesus Healing House Ministries...

Miracles Still Happen!

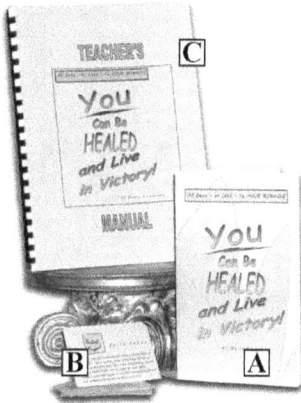

A. *"30 Days-Or-Less-To YOUR Miracle: You Can Be Healed and Live in Victory!"* by Holly Lewerenz. This interactive 32-page book includes a daily scripture, teaching on healing and victory for your life, and a prayer you can personalize to bring the results you need... $12

B. *Healing Scriptures* Faith Cards
This 40-pack of business-size cards is easy to carry anywhere and will keep the healing scriptures fresh in your mind, and ready at a moment's notice to fight off that negative thought that attacks you $7

C. *Healing Teacher's Manual*
This handy manual will be a helpful guide for you if you are a group leader using *"30 Days-Or-Less-To YOUR Miracle: You Can Be Healed and Live in Victory!"* as curriculum for your Bible study, healing class or other group. **FREE** with book "A" above.

D. *"Baptism of the Holy Spirit"* by Holly Lewerenz. Have you ever wondered about this experience which is talked about in the Bible? This book answers your questions and explains the mystery behind this wonderful gift from God. $12

♥ SPECIAL ♥
All 3 Products (ABD) $25

> **ORDER ONLINE AT**
> **www.JesusHealingHouse.org**

"Healing Is For YOU" Product Order Form

Don't miss receiving these life-changing products!

Fill out this form and mail to:

Jesus Healing House Ministries
P.O. Box 31883
Chicago, IL 60631

Name:_____
Address:_____
City:_____ State:____ Zip:_____
Phone:_____
Email:_____

	Quantity	$ Amount
A. *"30 Days-Or-Less-To YOUR Miracle: You Can Be Healed and Live in Victory!"* book / $12 ea.	_____	$_____
B. *Healing Scriptures* Faith Cards, 40-pack / $7 ea.	_____	$_____
C. *Healing Teacher's Manual* **FREE** *(quantity of one)*	1	$ FREE
D. *"Baptism of the Holy Spirit"* book / $12 ea.	_____	$_____
All 3 Products (A, B, D) $25	_____	$_____
TOTAL AMOUNT ENCLOSED: _____		$_____

Please use check or money order. You will receive your products in two to three weeks. Thank you!

www.ingramcontent.com/pod-product-compliance
Lightning Source LLC
LaVergne TN
LVHW051458080426
835509LV00017B/1811